THE
SECRET
OF THE
SPEAR

D1039599

By the same author

The Lost World of Agharti
The Hollow Earth Enigma

THE
SECRET
OF THE
SPEAR

THE MYSTERY
OF THE
SPEAR
OF LONGINUS

by

ALEC MACLELLAN

Souvenir Press

First published in Great Britain in 2004 by Souvenir Press Ltd
43 Great Russell Street, London WC1B 3PD

Copyright © 2004 by Alec Maclellan

The right of Alec Maclellan to be identified as the author of this
work has been asserted by him in accordance with the Copyright,
Designs and Patents Act 1988.

All rights reserved. No part of this publication may be reproduced,
stored in a retrieval system or transmitted, in any form or by any
means, electronic, mechanical, photocopying, or otherwise,
without the prior permission of the Copyright owner.

ISBN 0 285 63696 0

Typeset by FiSH Books, London
Printed and bound in Great Britain by
Cox & Wyman Ltd, Reading, Berks

Whosoever possesses this Spear and understands the powers it serves holds in his hands the destiny of the world for good or evil.

Old prophecy

Acknowledgements

The works of writers I have consulted during the writing of this book are acknowledged in the text, but I should also like to thank the following for their invaluable contributions to my research: Neville Armstrong, Dr Franz Kirchweger, Dr Robert Feather, Dr C.T. Davis, H.G.R. King, H. Kleinclausz, Nigel Pennick, Eugene Muntz, David Lang, Herbert Thurston, Laura Hibbard Loomis, Chris Scott, John Kent and Greta Erben. Members of the staff of the London Library, Wiener Library, Kunsthorisches Museum in Vienna and the Library of Congress in Washington. D.C. were also generous with their time and assistance. The British Newspaper Library, the Wiener Library, the Kunsthistoriches Museum and the British Museum kindly provided the photographs in the book; the remainder are from my own archives.

I am grateful to the following publishers, newspapers and magazines who have allowed me to quote from their publications. McGraw Hill for *The Occult and the*

Third Reich by Jean-Michel Angeburt; Neville Spearman and C.W. Daniel Co. for *The Spear of Destiny* by Trevor Ravenscroft and *Hitler's Secret Sciences* by Nigel Pennick; Thunderbird Press Inc. for *Adolf Hitler and the Secrets of the Holy Lance* by Howard A. Buechnner and Wilhelm Bernhardt; HarperCollins for *Satan and Swastika* by Francis King; Berkley Books for *Phantom Forces* by Richard Rainey; Temple Lodge Press for *The Ninth Century and the Holy Grail* by Walter Johannes Stein and Souvenir Press for *The Morning of the Magician* by Louis Pauwels and Jacques Bergier; *National Geographical Magazine, The Sunday Times, New Scientist, The Sunday Telegraph* and *The Guardian*. Extracts from the Authorised Version of *The Bible* (The King James Bible), the rights of which are vested in the Crown, are reproduced by permission of the Crown's Patentee, Cambridge University Press.

Contents

Illustrations

Line drawings

Prologue

'The Spear of Destiny ' has become an increasingly familiar phrase in the media. In fact, it has been generating public interest for some years because of appearances in operas like Richard Wagner's peerless medieval fantasy, *Parsifal*, where the good Knight, Sir Parsifal and the evil magician, Klingsor, battle for possession; or, alternately, in discussions about Picasso's magnificent anti-war painting, 'Guernica', in which some theorists have pointed out both the spear and a hidden image of Adolf Hitler.

In popular art and literature, too, the term has been used in films, comic books, on television, in video games and even pop music. In 1995, the all-action movie hero, Indiana Jones, encountered it in a four-part comic book series, *Indiana Jones and the Spear of Destiny*. Two years later on TV Michael Nankin's *The Spear of Destiny* placed the spear – which was said to have once belonged to a Roman centurion named Longinus present at the crucifixion of Jesus Christ – into the hands of a modern youngster, Conor, generating a powerful effect on the boy as well as all those with whom he comes into contact.

In the 1990s, 'The Spear of Destiny ' was a 'loud and brash' UK punk rock group founded by Nick Cash, whose music provided several best-selling albums, including the controversial Religion (1997). The record was followed by a video game that invited the player to take on the role of B. J. Blazkowicz, 'the Allies' most valuable agent in the Second World War'. The Spear of Destiny has been seized by the Nazis and placed in the impregnable Castle Wolfstein where Hitler plans to use its invincible power to sweep across Europe. The role-player's mission is to recapture the spear from an already unbalanced Hitler – or 'get ripped to pieces'.

For many people, 'The Spear of Destiny' is no more than this – an unbelievable fantasy with undertones of religion, the supernatural and the occult. For others it is the incredible story of an ancient relic believed to have amazing powers that has caused men to fight and die to own it for 2,000 years.

For those with an open mind, these are the facts behind the legend.

ALEC MACLELLAN
Dalyan, Turkey
October 2003

One

Judgement Day

The group of men crossing the Schillerplatz in Vienna on a grey, blustery January morning in 2003 have looks of expectancy and anxiety on their faces in equal measure. The party have emerged from the stately Kunsthistorisches Museum, one of the impressive buildings that form the magnificent cluster of the palatial Hofburg in the city centre, and now walk purposefully along the Opern Ring past the statue of the poet and dramatist, Friedrich Schiller, to the entrance of the Technische Universitat (Technical University), situated where the Schillerplatz adjoins the busy Getreide Markt.

None of the men, though, have time to appreciate the beautiful architecture in this area that at first glance can make the whole city seem like a gigantic museum, firmly resisting any ideas of modernisation or innovation. Nor do they appreciate the fact that the museums are probably unparalleled anywhere in the world for the eclectic nature of their contents, which display all aspects of human activity from crime to

pathology, dolls to clocks and alcohol to funeral rites –
all of which have been collected with what has been
described as a 'semi-spiritual fervour'.

The purpose of these men this morning combines
ancient legend with the very latest scientific
technology, for they are about to attempt to solve a
mystery that has endured for 2,000 years. They are
going to try to date an artefact that was allegedly in use
at the time of the crucifixion of Jesus Christ. It is an
experiment that has taken many months and much
careful negotiation to arrange.

One of the most concerned men in the group is Dr
Franz Kirchweger, a curator from the Kunsthistorisches
Museum, who is responsible for the relic and its safe
conduct to and from the Technical University. He is only
too well aware of all the stories surrounding it and how,
over the centuries, great men all over Europe are said to
have fought and died in their attempts to possess it:
Names from the distant past – Emperor Constantine
who used it to win the Battle of the Milvian Bridge,
Charlemagne who fought 47 campaigns with it by his
side, and Frederick Barbarossa whose empire was
founded on its power – and of recent time: Napoleon
Bonaparte, Winston Churchill and, most infamously of
all, Adolf Hitler.

Apart from the relic's religious significance – it
spilled the blood of the Son of God – some have
claimed that it also possesses mystical powers to shape
the destiny of its owner, and it has proved as important

Ancient spear – probably from the Carolingian era

to many of these people as Excalibur was to King Arthur. It is even regarded in certain quarters as a means of ruling the world.

As far as Dr Kirchweger, the man carrying the relic down the street clutched under his arm in a small oblong box, is concerned, he is in accord with the simple statement on the card in the glass case where it is displayed as Item 155 in Room 11 of the museum's *Schatzkammer* (Treasure House):

Heilige Lanze. Karolingisch, 8 Jh.
Mit spateren Erganzungen
Stahl, Eisen, Messing, Silber, Gold, Leder
(Inv.nr. XIII 19)
[Holy Lance, Carolingian, 8th century.
With later additions of
Steel, Iron, Brass, Silver, Gold, Leather]

The museum authorities have granted just six hours for the item to be removed from the case and tested by one of the world's leading metallurgists, Dr Robert Feather from England. Two security guards – their eyes never still as they make the short journey across the open square – accompanied by several journalists complete the party.

The last building they all pass before reaching their destination is the imposing, neo-Renaissance Akademie der Bildenden (Kunste Academy of Fine Art) erected on a site originally reserved for the Austrian parliament. None of the men probably gives a second thought to the fact that one of the people most closely associated with the spearhead they are about to test once tried to gain admission to the prestigious institution. His name was Adolf Hitler and as an eighteen-year-old he had applied for a place as a student in 1907. He had been refused on the grounds that his drawing of a human head was 'incompetent' and it was suggested he try architecture instead.

All the men are happy to get out of the chilly wind when they step into the Technical University. At the door, a porter, who has clearly been expecting Dr Kirchweger and his party, directs them to the Faculty for Metallurgy and Engineering. In a few minutes, they are all entering a spacious, neon-lit room packed with the very latest scientific equipment.

Dr Kirchweger wastes no time. Carefully he opens the box that he has carried from the museum and lifts out from some sheets of Japanese tissue paper the object of all this attention. It is a small, ornate spearhead, dark grey in colour, with a golden sheath around the middle. The curator places it almost reverently on the work surface and takes a step back. He will not let it out of his sight for an instant during the remainder of the morning.

Those who have never seen the relic before lean forward for a closer look. To all of them, it seems hardly possible that this curious but rather unprepossessing implement could have generated one of the most extraordinary legends in both religious and occult history and earned a variety of names including 'The Spear of Longinus', 'The Lance of St Maurice', '*Der Heilige Lanze*' (The Holy Lance), and, most recently, 'The Spear of Destiny'. But can it really be the weapon used by a Roman centurion to hasten the end of Christ, as described in the Bible?

Despite his outward calm, Dr Robert Feather is as excited as anyone about finally having a chance to examine the spearhead, so long parted from its wooden shaft. He has been aware of its existence for years and welcomed the invitation to bring his special skills to bear in a scientific attempt to discover just how old it might be. A metallurgist trained at London University, Dr Feather had been working as a technical engineering writer for twenty years contributing to metallurgical and electronic magazines as well as spending a good deal of time investigating comparative religions. In 1996, he became intrigued by the Dead Sea Scrolls after he had looked at a collection of old manuscripts and texts found in a synagogue, and now part of the Genizah Collection at Cambridge University. The scrolls, which had originally been found in 1947, were still baffling many experts and Dr Feather decided to investigate for himself. One of them – made of copper – particularly caught his attention. He recalled later:

> A lot of people had been looking into it from all different directions, but I thought I could come at it from a completely new angle. I could look with fresh eyes, completely unblinkered and with no rose-tints. I began to think, 'They're on the wrong track, and there are some basic, technological mistakes they are making.' So a fascinating story began to unravel.

Using his knowledge of metallurgy and drawing on his study of ancient Jewish and Middle Eastern history and religion, Dr Feather set about trying to decipher the characters engraved on the copper scroll. The results were sensational:

The fact the scroll was copper meant it was 2,000 years old and the people who wrote it wanted it to have some permanency. I discovered that it listed sixty-four locations where buried treasures were hidden, ranging from gold, silver, jewellery, garments, oils and other scrolls. And in coming to a translation of the text, I believe I've located some of those treasures listed in the Copper Scroll.

Having just completed a book about his discoveries, *The Copper Scroll Decoded*, Dr Feather was happy to accept the invitation to put his skills to work on the ancient spearhead that was said to date from the same era. Once again he brought to bear the same painstaking attention to detail and open-minded attitude to the spearhead that he had used on the copper scroll.

First, he weighed and measured the spearhead. It was 20 inches long, with the blade approximately 3 inches wide and $\frac{5}{8}$ inch thick (508 x 76 x 15mm). He worked on silently, noting the dark, battleship grey colour, the apparent sharpness of the edges, and then put it under a microscope to examine the component parts. This confirmed that the spearhead was made of steel, iron, brass, gold, silver and leather. Two wing-like blades were fixed to the lower end of the blade by thongs and a crisscross of wires. A number of small brass crosses had also been decoratively inlaid. Four more bands of silver wire bound up what had obviously been a break in the blade and were covered by a silver sheath.

In a recess of the blade, Dr Feather discovered what looked, intriguingly, like an iron pin or nail. The object was partly screened by the striking golden sheath that covered almost half the length of the spearhead and sparkled under the room's artificial lighting, but it was clear enough for him to read the inscription on the shaft that stated, *Lancea et clavus Domini* – 'Lance and nail of the Lord'.

Each of the tests that Dr Robert Feather carried out that morning had to be cleared with Dr Kirchweger before he could begin – and several produced their tricky moments. Prior to him applying some biological swabs to test for organic material such as blood, the curator insisted that a hairdryer be found. Once the dampened cotton had swabbed the relic, all traces of moisture had to be removed by the dryer before the investigation could continue.

Finally, under the watchful eyes of both the curator and Dr Feather, a radiographer carried out X-ray diffraction and fluorescence tests to reveal the structure and composition of the spearhead. Dr Feather then entered the mass of data and information he had collected into his pre-programmed computer for analysis. The results, which chattered out from the printer, provided more puzzles than answers.

There were no traces of blood or hair to be found on the spearhead that might link it to the crucifixion. The forensic test did, though, reveal a few skin cells and even some minute spores and particles – but nothing that could not have attached itself to the lance during its years on display in the Kunsthistonsches museum with a constant swirl of visitors all around it. The silver wire was shown to date from some time after AD 600, while the silver sheath had probably been fitted in the eleventh century. The brilliant gold sheath had been affixed some three centuries later still.

None of these facts proved that the spearhead – which had clearly been broken at some point in its history and subsequently repaired and strengthened – might not be old enough to have been made, or contain parts made, at the time of Christ. Certainly, it bore the marks of having been forged rather than moulded – clear evidence of the blacksmith's art – although in size it did seem to be rather bigger than those known to have been in use by the Roman army at this time. But it was the curious pin or nail in the recess that most puzzled Dr Feather, as he later explained to journalist Mary Ann Bird of *Time* magazine:

The iron pin – long claimed to be a nail from the crucifixion hammered into the blade and set off by tiny brass crosses – is consistent in length and shape with a first century Roman nail. While we cannot date the iron fragments around it, the crosses are significant. Someone used them to mark an area believed to contain parts of a nail used in the True Cross. We are in the realms of speculation, but you cannot rule it out. Some people have faith in it – and faith is a wondrous thing.

As a result of his tests in Vienna, Dr Feather is inclined to believe that the spearhead he examined was probably made sometime around the seventh century – a little earlier than estimated by the museum – and might just contain a fragment of a crucifixion nail incorporated into it. He does not believe it is a fake – as one particular story has claimed – created just over half a century ago. And he is amused by other rumours that the *real* spear is now either in the hands of the Americans where its power has enabled them to 'rule' the world, or hidden in Antarctica where it will be reclaimed in the fullness of time to help create the Fourth Reich.

But if there is one thought to emerge from this confusion of myths and theories, then it is surely this. Could there be more than one artefact bearing the name of 'The Spear of Destiny' located in different parts of the world? To find the answer, it is necessary to travel back in time to the fateful moment when the Roman centurion Longinus committed his immortal act and from there to follow the path of his spear down through history to the present day.

Two

The Man Who Stabbed the Messiah

It was the day that the veteran centurion had been expecting for weeks, even months. Ever since he had been ordered to follow the Jewish prophet across the wastelands and through the towns and villages of the countryside, keeping a watch on his activities and reporting back to his masters, he had somehow suspected that it might all end on a hill like this one on a Friday morning.

The man had seen crucifixions before, of course – the Romans had been using this form of punishment on criminals and enemies of the Roman State for over a century – but there was something unlike any other about this one. The figure who now hung on a wooden cross between two common thieves was extraordinary: while all three were racked with pain, the criminals showed little of *his* composure and bravery.

Gaius Cassius (as he is named in the apocryphal *Gospel of Nicodemus*) had been trailing this man for two years on the orders of Governor Pontius Pilate, the Pro-Consul of Roman-occupied Judaea. His name was Jesus of Nazareth and according to local gossip he was said to be the long-awaited Messiah As far as Pontius was concerned, he was preaching against the authority of Rome and represented a very real threat to law and order.

Over the months, the centurion had been sending reports of his observations to the Roman Pro-Consul. Although Gaius' eyesight was not good, he had seen nothing to implicate the man in any kind of terrorist activities. This man who called himself Jesus of Nazareth preached a message of love and understanding. To the centurion he appeared every inch a dedicated teacher, or rabbi, and he had never seen him raise so much as a finger in anger.

Even though Jesus had gathered a number of followers who were constantly around him and always attracted large crowds of men and women wherever he went, Gaius was in no doubt that the man knew that he was being followed. On more than one occasion when he had been speaking, Jesus had glanced with a smile of recognition to where he stood at the side or behind the crowds.

Spying on such a man had not been what Gaius Cassius had planned to do when he had joined the Legion in Rome as a young man. Both his father and grandfather had been soldiers and he wanted to follow in their footsteps. His wish had been granted and he had seen action under the banner of the eagle in the regions around Rome as well as across the seas to the East, and in Egypt.

Wherever he had been posted he was never without a spear which, according to the Gospel of Nicodemus, had originally been presented to his grandfather by Julius Caesar as a special award for the legionnaire's bravery in the conquest of Gaul. Known as a *hasta* (long spear) it had an iron head mounted on a hardwood shaft twice the length of his own body. Gaius' father had carried that same lance when he soldiered for Germanicus Caesar and then passed it on to him when he joined up. It seemed perpetually sharp, never rusted and because of its history, possessed almost magical qualities for its owner. It had certainly seen Gaius safely through a number of dangerous situations prior to his final posting in Judaea.

It had been as a result of developing cataracts in both his eyes – probably caused by the years of fighting in the harsh sunlight and dust storms of the deserts of the Middle East – that his soldiering days had come to an end. But he had been a loyal and dedicated soldier to his country and a job was found for him in the strife-torn land of the Jews – a free-ranging assignment to report on the religious and political scene in Jerusalem and the surrounding districts. In the main it had been an easy task. The rabbi Jesus had made no attempt to hide his presence and indeed the sheer numbers of people who followed him – or stood waiting for him to speak – made keeping him in sight not too difficult even for someone with his poor vision. It was also not difficult to be present at what he knew would be the final hours of the man's life, bringing his mission to an end.

Cassius had, in fact, been an eyewitness to almost every moment of the drama following the arrest of Jesus. He had been present the previous day when Jesus was tried before the Sanhedrin and had even flinched when a soldier struck him across the face for remaining silent while being questioned by Caiaphas, the High Priest. The next morning, he had risen as the sun came up to see the battered and bruised figure taken across Jerusalem to the Praetorium of the Fortress Antonia, Pontius Pilate's seat of government. Again Jesus had remained silent, as Cassius' master, Pontius, had shifted the responsibility for the *rabbi*'s inevitable execution to Herod, the King of Judaea. Later, the centurion had listened to the shouts of the mob outside the Praetorium when Pontius had ordered the release of the robber, Bar-abbas, and condemned Jesus to a scourging and crucifixion.

Crucifixion, he knew, had long been considered such a humiliating form of punishment that it was never used on Roman citizens, only for slaves or people considered beneath the dignity of Roman citizenship. The complication, which arose where Jesus was concerned, was that under Jewish law no man could be executed on the Sabbath Day – especially before Passover. Indeed, if a prisoner were still alive as darkness fell, it was required of the Roman authorities to ensure a prompt death, usually by breaking both the victim's

2. Drawing of longinus and his spear from an old fresco

legs. Pilate had no hesitation in agreeing to such a
demand in the case of Jesus, particularly as he was as
anxious to prove to the Judaeans that the man was no
Messiah, merely a heretic of skin and bone like
themselves.

A Roman legionnaire – much like Gaius himself –
had performed the scourging, stripping off the
prisoner's clothes and tying his hands to a post above

his head, then lashing him across the shoulders, back and legs with a *Flagrum* – a short whip consisting of several thongs with two small balls of lead attached to the end of each. Even from where he stood watching through weak eyes, Gaius could see the lacerated flesh and terrible bruising that left Jesus more dead than alive by the time the officer-in-charge ordered the beating to stop.

There followed an awful scene when the Roman soldiers taunted the man who claimed to be the Jews' king – throwing a robe across his shoulders and placing a crown of thorns, made from some small branches kept for lighting fires, around his forehead. The veteran legionnaire also saw the robe torn from the prisoner's back – wrenching off strips of flesh and clots of blood – and the heavy patibulum of the cross tied across his shoulders.

Gaius did not move as Jesus and the two other prisoners, later apparently named as Gestas and Dismas, were lined up to begin their journey to Golgotha, 'The Place of the Skulls'. At the head of the group were the Temple Guards carrying Herod's spear. This was the symbol of their power to perform the crucifixion: an act which the Roman soldiers and their centurion did not have the authority to carry out on their own.

As the execution party moved off on the 650-yard journey from Fortress Antonia to Golgotha, Gaius could tell that every step was excruciating agony for Jesus. He saw him stumble and fall on several occasions and then finally slump into the dust. A man in the crowd – who the centurion would learn later was Simon of Cyrene from North Africa – was pulled out of the throng by the Roman centurion and ordered to carry the cross for the last few yards of its journey.

Once on Golgotha, Jesus was shown one solitary act of kindness by his executioners, according to some Biblical sources. He was offered a pain-relieving mixture of wine and myrrh, but refused to take it. Seeing this, one of the men gave a shrug of his shoulders and pushed Jesus backwards on to the cross. With practised ease, he drove a wrought-iron nail through each of the prisoner's hands. Gaius watched as the cross was lifted into position. The Roman then placed Jesus' left foot over his right foot and drove a third iron nail through the arch of both feet into the wood beneath.

Only when this was over was Gaius aware that the guards had nailed a notice on the top of the cross, 'The King of the Jews'. Even as he read it, he saw the man beneath sag down on the nails piercing his palms as if he had neither the strength nor the inclination to do otherwise. The old soldier knew that even if Jesus did try to push himself up to relieve the weight on his arms, the pain in his feet and throughout the rest of his body would only be made worse.

For some time, Gaius Cassius stood lost in thought. He had never seen such courage and dignity before on the face of anyone who had been crucified. He was in no doubt that this extraordinary man whom he had followed for so long would die soon, but he was unable to tear himself away. He could see, vividly, the effort it took Jesus to push his body upwards to gulp breath into his lungs and heard, unmistakably, the words he spoke during his last moments.

The centurion watched as Jesus looked down on the Roman soldiers beneath the cross gambling for his clothes, and heard him say, 'Father, forgive them for they know not what they do.' Turning to the penitent thief beside him he spoke the words, 'Today, you shall be with me in Paradise.' Then, glancing down, he addressed the group of women around Mary, his mother, 'Woman, behold your son.' To one of his followers, John, who stood by their side, he whispered, 'Behold your mother.' It was the crucified man's next cry which echoed across the bleak hillside of Golgotha that seared into Gaius Cassius' mind and remained with him for the rest of his life, 'My God, My God, why have You forsaken Me?'

Agonising pain was obviously piling upon Jesus when – as the disciples Matthew and Luke were to describe later – there was 'darkness over the earth.'

Still the Roman could not bring himself to leave, even when the dying man's breathing grew even shallower. Then Gaius Cassius heard another strangled cry, 'I thirst.' At that moment, he would almost have stepped forward himself but for one of the guards putting up a sponge soaked in *posca* – a cheap, sour wine that had been the staple diet of all legionnaires, himself included – to Jesus' lips. This time he took a sip. There was a pause, then: 'It is finished.'

In fact, the terrible drama was not quite over. Summoning up one last surge of strength, Jesus pushed his torn feet against the nail which penetrated them both, and cried out a last time, 'Father, into Your hands I commit My spirit.'

If the guards around the cross were aware of these final words they gave no indication. Instead, they prepared to carry out the last act of the crucifixion before darkness fell: the crurifracture – breaking the legs of the men on the cross so that they could not push themselves upwards any more and relieve the muscles of their chests. Rapid suffocation would immediately follow, Gaius Cassius knew.

The legs of Gestas and Dismas were brutally smashed by soldiers who had performed the act many times before. But as one of them moved towards Jesus, the figure in the shadow of the cross who had watched the events all day, at last intervened. Gaius took a firm hold of his grandfather's spear and stepped forward. Without a moment's hesitation he drove it between the fourth and fifth ribs of the man who had scarcely been out of his sight for the past two years.

Now it *was* over.

But a legend had just begun . . .

According to the Gospel of John, 19:34: 'One of the

soldiers with a spear pierced his side, and forthwith came there out blood and water.' This is fairly conclusive evidence that Gaius Cassius' thrust was through the pericardium and into the heart, causing the flow of watery fluid from the sac surrounding the heart and the blood of the interior of the heart. It would indicate, too, that Jesus died not from the usual crucifixion death of suffocation but heart failure, due to shock and constriction of the heart by fluid in the pericardium.

Such a medical explanation would have been far beyond the understanding of the man whose simple motive had been to put the crucified man out of his misery. Whether Cassius left the scene of his act of mercy then, or waited for the bodies to be taken down from the crosses immediately as was required by law, is not recorded.

What is known is that Herod's spear – which had lent authority to the crucifixion – was soon being carried back to the Temple in Jerusalem where Caiaphas and the other priests awaited the news that the troublesome 'Messiah' was no more. The authority it symbolised would pass with that of its owner, however, while such fame as it had would soon be far overshadowed by the spear that Gaius Cassius had used to stab the dying Christ. That spear was destined for a quite different fate.

It has to be admitted that much of the evidence about the life of Gaius Cassius is based on hearsay and incomplete records – though the central facts of his presence at the crucifixion of Jesus Christ and his action with the spear are beyond doubt. The rest of the information about him is, nevertheless, well worth examining in order to help piece together the subsequent history of the centurion's remarkable spear.

That he was no hard-hearted soldier, but a man of strong emotions moved by what he saw that day at Golgotha seems very evident. Certainly his actions speak of someone who did not want to see the same mutilation that had been meted out to the two thieves being done to the courageous Jesus – and so he stepped forward to show that the man was already dead by a quick thrust of his spear into the chest. Such an action was, in fact, quite common among Roman soldiers to demonstrate that an enemy who had fought well on the battle-field was already dead and should be spared any further indignity.

There is, sadly, no information as to where Gaius Cassius was born, though it has been suggested in some quarters that he may have been of Germanic extraction Certainly he came from a soldiering family and took in military lore 'with his mother's milk'. He must have served what was known as the 'enlistment' period of twelve years that was required of all legionaries. After this – if a man survived the rigours and dangers of the common soldier's lot – he could hope to be commissioned as a centurion. Gaius' impressive list of campaigns indicates that he had certainly served his time, was probably highly thought of, and instead of being invalided out was given a job in espionage.

The act of mercy that he performed on Golgotha soon came to be regarded by Jesus' followers as proof that their leader was the Messiah. It fulfilled two of the prophecies laid down by Zechariah in the Old Testament that would confirm His coming: 'Not one bone of his will be broken,' and 'They will look on him whom they have pierced.'

The crucifixion clearly had a very traumatic effect on Gaius Cassius whose name was not, in fact, known until it later appeared in verse 7:8 of the *Gospel of Nicodemus* (formerly called the *Acts of Pontius Pilate* and written in the sixth century) and also in the writings of the Greek patriarch, Germanus, in 715 – which might explain the idea that he was Germanic. Both sources, though, are mistaken in calling him Longinus, which is almost certainly latinised from the Greek word Longche, meaning a spear. It was later writers who combined this word and his real name when referring to him as Gaius Cassius Longinus.

It is evident, too, that folklore and legend were soon busy with the life story of the centurion and the fate of 'The Spear of Longinus', as it became known. All these sources are, though, agreed that, as a result of his experiences, the Roman centurion became a convert to Christianity – inspired by the events he witnessed and the ominous eclipse of the sun that occurred before Jesus' death.

One account of his conversion says that immediately Gaius had pierced Jesus' body, he fell to his knees before the cross. As he looked up, some of the blood and lymph from the body dripped on to his eyes and his sight was miraculously restored. According to both Matthew (27:54) and Mark (15:39), the Roman exclaimed, 'Indeed, this was the Son of God' while Luke (23:47) actually quotes him as declaring: 'Truly, this was an upright man.'

Immediately after the crucifixion, Gaius went to Fortress Antonia and requested Pontius to relieve him of his duties. After leaving the army, he sought out some of those he had seen following Jesus and spent several months learning about his teachings. Gaius later became a monk in the ancient Roman city of Mazarca in Cappadocia – on the site of the present-day town of Kayseri in Turkey – and then travelled widely preaching the message of Christianity. Clutched in his right hand, firming his resolve and inspiring his mission, was the fateful spear.

Another legend of Gaius Cassius maintains that he soon fell foul of the law – just as Jesus had done. Now it became his turn to be spied upon and arrested and taken before the authorities in Caesarea. He, too, resisted all the tortures to make him deny his new faith, even after all his teeth had been extracted and his tongue cut out. Despite this – the story says – Gaius was still able to speak and used his spear to smash a number of pagan idols before of the Roman governor's astonished gaze.

This particular piece of hagiography also provides a version of Gaius' death and martyrdom. For it is said that as he broke the idols, a number of demons that had been living in them escaped and attacked the governor, depriving him of his sight and driving him mad. At this, the centurion informed the unfortunate man writhing at his feet that he would only regain his sight when he, Gaius Cassius, was dead. On hearing this, the governor apparently regained some of his composure and ordered an immediate execution. The legend concludes:

> And the governor ordered him to be beheaded. When his head fell from his body, some of his blood splashed into the governor's eyes and his sight was immediately restored. At this miracle, the governor was converted to the Christian faith just as Longinus had been at the crucifixion of Christ.

Following his death, the story of Gaius Cassius Longinus becomes even stranger. Sabine Baring-Gould, the Anglican clergyman and composer of the famous hymn, 'Onward, Christian Soldiers', made a particular study of his life for his definitive volume of *The Lives of the Saints* published in 1914. In between his duties as a parish priest in Devon, Baring-Gould became fascinated by the links between mythology and theology and combed many ancient documents for the facts about his subjects, in particular the Roman spearman. He was not impressed by the earlier anonymous work The Latin Acts of Saint Longinus, which seemed to pile improbability upon impossibility, as he made clear in his entry in *The Lives of the Saints*:

> It is pretended that the body of S. Longinus was found at Mantua in 1304, together with the sponge stained with Christ's blood, wherewith he had assisted in cleansing our Lord's body when it was taken down from the cross. These relics have been distributed in various places. Parts are in Prague, others in Carlstein, the body in the Vatican at Rome. But the Sardinians assert that they possess the body of S. Longinus, which was found in their island, where he suffered under Nero. And the Greeks say he suffered in Gabala in Cappadocia. The head is, however, also said to have been found in Jerusalem and carried into Cappadocia.

While it is clear from this that the whereabouts of the body of Gaius Cassius Longinus will probably never be known, the passage of the spear that pierced the side of Christ *is* better documented. It is a trail that continues in an unlikely spot high up in the glorious mountain range of the Swiss Alps and concerns an amazing band of soldiers known as 'The Thundering Legion'.

Three

St Maurice and the Theban Legion

There are two roads that follow the winding River Rhône as it cuts through the Swiss Alps on its course to Italy. There is the direct N9 toll motorway that will enable the driver from Geneva with business to attend to in Milan or further south to make good time along his way; or, alternatively, the gently meandering older highway No. 9, which enters the mountains at Chillon and passes in the shadow of the towering 14,691-foot-high peak of the Matterhorn to re-enter the lowlands again on the shore of Lake Maggiore.

The more leisurely route through the Valais canton is the one to pursue by the motorist intent on enjoying the spectacular scenery of the Rochers de Naye, a glimpse of the Pas des Morgans or views of the aptly named Les Diablerets. His is, in fact, following a highway that men have used to cross one frontier to another for centuries from the days of the Romans and even earlier. On it, too, he can visit one of the earliest localities associated with 'The Spear of Destiny'.

The sign to look for is that of the town of St

Maurice, which is found about three kilometres south of the bustling centre of Bex, in a narrow section of valley framed by the Dents du Midi (10,628ft) on one side and the Dent de Morcles (9,741ft) on the other. The ancient town is not difficult to spot as it stands at a point where the Rhône narrows and the Romans were prompted to build a bridge when on one of their earliest marches of conquest to the north. This imposing structure is the first clue that here is a place steeped in history. The second lies in its name.

St Maurice commemorates a warrior saint who was martyred nearby in AD 287. The story of the terrible fate he suffered may not be as well known today as it deserves, but his name can be found all over the world. At the last count there were 598 churches, 74 towns and four cathedrals named after him, not forgetting two entire countries, Mauritania and Mauritius – after the Latin for his name. The Roman emperor who ordered his murder and saw it carried it out with dreadful savagery is, appropriately, largely forgotten.

During Roman times, St Maurice was known as Aguanum and because of its position was made the first capital of the region and served as an important communications centre. Weary legionaries passed through on their way back from battles in western Europe, with fresh troops going in the other direction to quell the pagan hordes rampaging across France and Germany.

At the head of one of these groups of men was a commander named Mauritius who carried with him an unusual lance. His fate near the picturesque little town would launch a legend that would earn both him and the locality a unique place in history.

The spot where the commander and his men defied the orders of their emperor and paid the price with their lives was beside a rocky cliff on the banks of the Rhône. A little over half a century later, the remains of Mauritius, and several of his officers including Candidus, Exuperius and Vitalis, were discovered by Theodore, the Bishop of Octodurum (now the nearby town of Martigny), who had heard of their martyrdoms. About the year 350 he erected a basilica against the cliff to mark the bloody event. The remains of this shrine are still visible in the Romanesque abbey that was subsequently built in 515 on land donated by King Sigismund of Burgundy. (For several centuries the Burgundian kings also made the town their main residence.) Today, the building, which has seen many alterations and reconstructions, is Switzerland's most ancient Christian site and the oldest surviving abbey north of the Alps.

The Abbaye de St-Maurice became a centre for pilgrims and has attracted visitors from all over Europe bringing gifts of gold and silver and a variety of magnificent medieval caskets and relics. Among these are the splendid gold cloisonne 'Casket of Teuderic', a beautiful filigreed silver 'Arm of St Bernard', and a remarkable silver bust of St Candidus, the officer who was also made a saint as a result of the events in AD 287. A medieval gold water jug given by Charlemagne is of

3 A relic of St Maurice from the abbaye de St Maurice

particular interest to those following the legend of the holy spear.

The cult of St Maurice has since spread throughout Switzerland, along the Rhône and into northern Italy and celebrated with its own feast day on 22 September. A liturgy to mark this day, the *laus perennis* ('Perpetual Praise') was commissioned from Constantinople and is still sung regularly at the abbey.

But at the very heart of the story of Maurice and his legionnaires lies a mystery. *What* happened to the spear that he was known to take with him everywhere he went and which inspired him to defy the might of Roman law?

★

There is considerable argument as to what occured to his spear after the death of Gaius Cassius Longinus at the hands of the Roman governor in Caesarea. One legend suggests it was seized by Herod who had heard about the Roman centurion's miraculous recovery of his sight. The cruel and ambitious king of Judaea was apparently anxious that anything which might suggest the divinity of Jesus should be impounded and destroyed. If this were the case, then he patently failed.

Another story claims that the lance came into the possession of Joseph of Arimathaea, the wealthy Jew and member of the Sanhedrin who was a secret supporter of Jesus. On the evening of the crucifixion he had asked Pontius Pilate for the dead man's body and gave it a decent burial in his own tomb – an act for which Christianity has always honoured him.

According to this account, Joseph took the cup from which Jesus drank at the Last Supper and brought it to Golgotha. When Longinus stabbed the body, he caught some of the blood in the vessel and created what has since been known throughout history as the 'Holy Grail'. The Rev. Ebenezer Cobham Brewer, who scoured Europe and investigated countless traditions in order to write his classic *Dictionary of Phrase and Fable* (1870) has written that Joseph was in possession of both the cup and the spear for a number of years:

Legend has in that Joseph was imprisoned for 12 years and was kept alive miraculously by the Holy

Grail and that on his release by Vespasian, *c.* 63, he brought the Grail and the spear with which Longinus wounded the crucified Saviour to Britain, founded the Abbey of Glastonbury whence he commenced the conversion of Britain.

In recounting how Joseph and his progeny became the guardians of the Holy Grail in England in the years which followed, Brewer also cites another fascinating piece of folklore concerning the two relics:

> Joseph of Arimathea brought to Listenise the sanctgraal and also the spear with which Longinus pierced the Saviour. When Sir Balin entered his chamber, which was in the palace of King Pellam, he found it 'marvellously well dight and richly; the bed was arrayed with cloth of gold, the richest that might be bought, and thereby stood a table of clean gold, with four pillars of silver, and upon the table stood the spear strangely wrought (*The History of Prince Arthur*, Part I, Chapter 40.)

As I shall reveal in the next chapter, there is a tradition of the spear being in Britain, but almost 900 years after this date. It is also stated in the account that the holy relic reached the country from mainland Europe. Nevertheless, the story about Joseph is an interesting one and another example of the rumours and myths that quickly began to surround the spear.

It has even been suggested that the spear might have been passed from one soldier to the next after Gaius Cassius resigned from the Roman Legion. He would have been expected to hand over his military tunic, armour and weapons and as a spear was standard Legion equipment, it might have been given to another legionnaire. But considering the special history of the weapon in his family, it seems highly unlikely that he would have parted with it under any circumstance.

What there *is* evidence of is the spear coming into the possession of the officer Mauritius. The best account of his life we have, the *Passio Martyrum Acaunensium* (The Passion of the Martyrs of Aguanum) written by the fifth-century French bishop, Eucherius of Lyon, says that Mauritius knew its history and believed in its power of destiny. Its symbolism helped underpin his faith when he decided to refuse to obey orders from his superior officer, Emperor Marcus Aurelius Maximian.

The bishop tells us nothing of Mauritius' early life and has no comment to make on a rumour that he was a direct descendant of the family of Gaius Cassius who had passed the spear down the generations – which is most unlikely. In his account, we first meet Mauritius in the spring of 286 when he was put in command of the Theban Legion, the *Alkateeba al Teebia* (alternately, the *Alksteeba al-sa'eedia*). These men were so named because they had all been conscripted in

Thebes in Upper Egypt and were unique in that every soldier was a Christian.

The actual number of men who signed up for the Theban Legion has been a matter of dispute – the figure varies from a few thousand to over 6,600 in the majority of accounts – but there is no argument that the area from which they came had a reputation for almost fanatical Christianity. Earlier generations had suffered terrible persecution with great fortitude and obeyed their priests, known as 'The Desert Fathers', without question.

For some months this new legion was quartered in the east, training under their commander, Mauritius, and his lieutenants, Candidus, the *senator militum* (first commanding officer) and Experius, his second lieutenant. Then they received orders from Maximian, the emperor of the Roman Commonwealth, who was jointly in charge of the empire with Gaius Diocletian. They were to march to Gaul where they would be required to help quash an uprising of rebels. Bishop Eucherius sets the scene for the drama that was to follow in the *Passio Martyrum Acaunensium*, apparently basing his facts on an oral account by a fourth-century bishop:

Here is the story of the passion of the Holy Martyrs who have made Aguanum illustrious with their blood. It is in honour of this heroic martyrdom that we narrate with our pen the order of events as it came to our ears. We often hear, do we not, a particular locality or city is held in high honour because of one single martyr who died there, and quite rightly, because in each case the saint gave his precious soul to the most high God. How much more should this sacred place, Aguanum, be reverenced, where so many thousands of martyrs have been slain, with the sword, for the sake of Christ?

After Emperor Maximian's summons the Theban legionaries sailed from Egypt to Rome and then marched across northern Italy to what is now called the St Bernard Pass. As the lines of men headed past towns and villages towards their appointment with destiny, their armour flashed so brightly in the sunlight and their feet pounded so hard on the ground that the sight of them earned the epithet, 'The Thundering Legion'.

The mighty unit of Egyptian soldiers crossed the pass and encamped near Aguanum to await orders from Emperor Maximian, who was already in position with his army at Octudurum. It was only when the Theban legionaries reached camp that they learned that they were to attack a group of rebel Christian peasants, known as the 'Bagaude', and that their mission was to assist in wiping out Christianity in Gaul.

Nor was that all. They were also expected to join with the rest of the emperor's soldiers in making offerings to the Roman gods to ensure victory – a routine enough procedure among the legions, but one recognising the emperor's claim to divinity. At this, according to Bishop Eucherius, 'Mauritius stood before his men and, brandishing the spear of Longinus, reminded them of Him who had died by it, and told them it would be a sin to fight their brethren.'

The great roar of approval that greeted this proclamation was followed by a decision of all the men to remain in camp and refuse to fight. Mauritius feared the outcome of this decision – and his fear proved well founded.

As soon as news of the Theban's decision reached the emperor he sent a message by return threatening the most dreadful reprisals if the men did not obey his command. Twice Mauritius replied that his men could not deny their faith. Then came the communication he feared most: if they did not comply, Maximian would decimate his army – one in every ten men would be executed. And if this order were not obeyed, a second, similar, slaughter would follow.

The faith of 'The Thundering Legion' was about to be tested to the full, as another account of the drama in the classic *Book of Martyrs* (1554) by the English martyrologist, John Foxe, describes:

The names of the soldiers were written on papers and placed in the helmets of the Centurions, for 600 were destined to perish as examples. These embraced their comrades, who encouraged them and even envied their fate. The plain soon flowed with the blood of the martyrs. The survivors persisted in declaring themselves Christians and the butchery began again; the blood of another 600 reddened the waters of the Rhône. This second severity made no more impression than the first had done. The soldiers preserved their fortitude and their principles, but by the advice of their officers they drew up a loyal remonstrance to the emperor.

The first chronicler of the massacre, Bishop Eucheris, managed to obtain details of this speech which he reprinted it in his book. It is an extraordinary mixture of faith, loyalty and bravery in equal parts:

Emperor, we are your soldiers, but also the soldiers of the true God. We owe you military service and obedience, but we cannot renounce Him who is our Creator and Master, and also yours even though you reject Him. In all things which are not against His law, we most willingly obey you, as we have done hitherto We readily oppose your enemies whoever they are, but we cannot stain our hands with the blood of innocent Christians. We have taken an oath to God before we took one to you and you cannot place any confidence in our second oath if we violate the first. You command us to execute Christians, behold we are such. We confess God the Father the creator of all things and His Son Jesus Christ. We have seen our comrades slain with the sword, we do not weep for them but rather rejoice at their honour. Neither this, nor any other provocations, has tempted us to revolt. Behold, we have arms in our hands but we do not resist, because we would rather die innocent than live by any sin.

Quite unmoved by this declaration, Maximium sent one final warning to the Thebans, telling them, 'Do not trust in your numbers, for if you persist in your refusal, not a man among you will survive.' When this, too, found Mauritius and his men unshakable in their resolve, a large host of the emperor's troops were ordered to march into Aguanum on 22 September 286 and slaughter every single soul. Not a sword was raised in defence: even the spear of Longinus remained at Mauritius' side as he, too, was cut down by a single blow of a sword.

The story did not quite end with the massacre at Aguanum. There were also some other members of 'The Thundering Legion' away from the area at the time – a number posted on guard duty along the road across the alps and beyond. But they were also all hunted down mercilessly by Maximium's men and put to the sword like their colleagues.

It was not long before rumours began to circulate that a number of miracles had occurred in the district in the aftermath of the massacre. The bodies of some of the Thebans that had been thrown into the Rhône were apparently seen by people rising from the water and praying on the riverbank. Beheaded figures had been seen walking in the valley with their hands clasped in prayer. Such was the impression left by these tales that Bishop Theodore chose the spot on the river bank for the site of his basilica – and excavations in the area in the 1940s unearthed a number of remains that require further investigation.

Today, the town of St Maurice is a peaceful place. Only the gold and silver relics in the abbey mark one of the bloodiest massacres in history. It is from them that one begins to get a sense of how the legend of the holy spear took hold of human imagination.

Four

Cult of the Spear

Brunanburh is a name to conjure with for those with a love of ancient history, a place with more than a touch of mystery about itself and also its precise location in England. It is, in fact, the earliest spot in the country to be associated with the legend of the holy spear and the location of a battle in 937 where the weapon is alleged to have played a crucial role.

The Battle of Brunanburh is recorded in the ancient *Anglo-Saxon Chronicles* as well as being celebrated in a famous poem by Alfred, Lord Tennyson. It is also the subject of a resounding claim by a man who figures large in our story, Winston Churchill. The great British prime minister said that the English owe their very existence as a nation to just three battles in history – the first of which was fought at Brunanburh by King Athelstan.

The facts about King Athelstan and his famous victory are well enough recorded – it is just the place where he defeated the combined Scottish, Welsh and Viking forces with the aid of the spear that remains elusive. However, as a result of my researches, I believe that this important battlefield was near the coast of Lancashire, in the shadow of the ancient Forest of Bowland. So how did the spear come to feature in this crucial moment of history? Where had it passed along the way?

King Athelstan was born in Wessex in 895, the son of King Edward the Elder and grandson of Alfred the Great. There is, however, some question as to his legitimacy, as his mother, Egwina, was believed to have been the daughter of a peasant shepherd with whom Edward fell in love. Most historical references mention her simply as 'a noblewoman', but there is no doubt of her beauty or her devotion to her son, Athelstan.

The boy apparently learned to read and write at an early age and like the children of all Anglo-Saxon noblemen, was instructed in the art of fighting. Shortly before his famous grandfather died in 899, Athelstan, according to a contemporary account, was presented to the old man who 'affectionately embraced him and gave him a Saxon sword, a jewelled scabbard, a belt and cloak'. By the time he was crowned king of the Mercians and Anglo-Saxons at Kingston-upon-Thames on 2 August 924, Athelstan had proved himself a skilled and courageous warrior.

The new king was a man of great ambition, too, determined to push the boundaries of his kingdom further than anyone before him, and he set about conquering portions of Cornwall, Wales and

4 A cross from the collection of King Athelstan

Northumbria. There were, however, rival forces growing fearful and resentful of his power who drew together in an unholy alliance: Constantine II the king of Scotland and Anlaf, the Viking king of Dublin. These men were angered by Athelstan's intention of becoming 'the first to rule what previously many kings shared between them' and, with their superior armies, plotted his downfall.

In the year 937, this coalition of enemies assembled on the British mainland. The Celts sent word that they would defy the Saxon 'palefaces' – as they called Athelstan and his followers – and crush them once and for all in a 'gigantic battle'. The odds were certainly stacked against Athelstan, but the brave and ambitious king set off for the encounter clasping an implement that he told his troops would ensure them victory – a holy spear that had pierced the side of Christ and made its owner invincible.

Athelstan had, in fact, been a keen collector of ancient artefacts and religious relics ever since the generous gift he had been given by his grandfather when he was six. Indeed, his reputation as a connoisseur had grown over the intervening years and many of the items in his possession had been imported from abroad, according to the evidence in the volumes of *Historia Monasterii Croylandenis*. This work indicates that a considerable number of his most prized possessions had been exchanged with other European monarchs.

The famous English chronicler, William of Malmesbury whose *Gesta Regum Anglorum* (1128) provides a history of the kings of England from the days of the Saxon invasion, claims that the 'holy lance' was given to King Athelstan by Hugo Capet, the founder of the third Frankish dynasty. This, however, is unlikely, as Capet was only a child in 937 – although the suggestion is that the spear was transported across the Channel to its new owner that same year.

Thomas Carlyle, the Victorian historian, in an essay 'Early Kings of Norway', also puts forward the theory that the spear could have been a gift from Harald Haarfagr, King of Norway, in return for a 'magnificent sword, with gold hilt and fine trimmings' sent by Athelstan as a mark of respect. This, too, seems improbable – and if there was a donor at this time, then it is more likely to have been the German, Heinrich I.

In any event, it is said that Athelstan carried the spear, resplendent with his colours, into the Battle of Brunanburh. The battle is said to have been fought over a thirty-mile front, according to the *Anglo-Saxon Chronicles*, from which the following information is extracted:

in this year, King Athelstan, Lord of Warriors, ring-giver to men, and his brother also, Prince Edmund, won eternal glory in battle with sword edges around Brunanburh. The enemy perished and there lay many a warrior by spear destroyed, Northern men shot over shield, likewise Scottish as well.

The saga goes on to describe how the remnants of the defeated armies fled across the sea to Ireland or back to Scotland, pursued for much of the way by Athelstan' s victorious men. Later the battle was recorded in Irish and Scottish annals and by the twelfth-century Welsh historian, Geoffrey of Monmouth, in his *Historia Regum Britaniae* (*c.* 1147). In it, he describes the battle as 'a turning point for the Celts'.

But *where* did this turning point in history take place? Over the years, historians have suggested a number of locations that range from the Solway Firth to Bridgnorth in Shropshire. Other candidates have included Doncaster, the area around the mouth of the Humber, the flatlands of Lincolnshire, even the south west of England. None of these, though, fit the interior clues of the Anglo-Saxon poem or the words of a saga writer named Egil Skallagrimsson to match the landscape around the small Lancashire market town of Garstang, which developed where the great north–south main road crosses the River Wyre.

Skallagrimsson was actually a member of Athelstan's court at the time of the battle and an eyewitness to the drama. He confirms that the king rode into battle brandishing the holy spear 'which struck his enemies with fear'. Being an Icelander by birth, the author understandably misspells some of the names in his account, but frequently refers to the location as *Vinuskogi*. In Norse, 'Vinu' means wood or heath, while 'skogi' is a phrase still existing in the name of an actual place, Myerscough, just to the south of Garstang. Records indicate that there was a forested area here in the Middle Ages, probably even earlier. The very name itself derives from the Saxon word 'Gaerstrung' meaning meadowland.

Further confirmation the battle site was here can be found in the famous *Book of Hengest*, which places the battle at 'Cattybrunawc.' This lies between Caterall and Hampson Green, not far from the ruins of Garstang Castle and the River Wyre where it runs north –

precisely as Skallagrimsson mentions in his description of King Athelstan riding out to confront his destiny.

Human remains have subsequently been found in and around the Wyre. These could be the bodies of defeated soldiers from Ireland who were trying to get back to their long ships on the river estuary at the same time as the Scots were retreating up an old Roman road going north. Interestingly, there is a place named 'Athelston Fold' beside this road between Preston and Fulwood and it has been suggested this could have been where the king and his men assembled for the great battle.

The scale of Athelstan's triumph – 'never was there more slaughter on this island' the poem states unequivocally, 'since from the east, Angles and Saxons came up over the broad sea' – causing the king's fame to spread even wider. He was not slow in striking victory coins bearing his likeness and the words *Rex Totius Britaine* (King of All Britain). He also took to coining flamboyant phrases in order to describe his new status such as '*basileus* of the English and in like manner ruler of the whole orb of Britain'.

As a result of Athelstan's victory, the country that had previously been a mix of Anglo-Saxon kingdoms now became unified. The borders, too, became those which have remained to this day.

The triumphant king demanded huge levies of gold, silver and precious artefacts from the defeated Welsh and Scots and also removed the Vikings from York where their fortress was destroyed and their treasures seized. The prize items were added to his own collection, while the rest were presented to the Church in order to gain the support of the clergy.

Pride of place in Athelstan's collection, though, went to the spear that had been by his side throughout the battle. Talk of its supernatural power was now widespread and the astute monarch put it on display for a time as a symbol of his power: first, at his northern headquarters in York, then later at Kingston-upon-Thames for the people of the south to have a chance to see.

Although he never married, King Athelstan worked hard to forge links with Europe by marrying off four of his half-sisters to various rulers in Western Europe. One of these unions was to prove particularly significant in the legend of the holy spear.

Shortly before his death at Gloucester on 27 October 939, Athelstan brokered the marriage of his half-sister Edith to the German king, Otto I, later Otto the Great. As part of her dowry – the story goes – the king had his precious spear transported by a troop of his most trusted soldiers to Mainz and presented to Otto. There was a condition attached to the gift, however: the emperor was to declare his garrison towns as trading cities and allow British merchants access to them. It was to prove a shrewd decision for both men. Athelstan ensured the support of his merchant classes, while Otto became known as 'The Town Founder' and helped the economy of Europe to emerge from the Dark Ages.

The deal also saw the holy lance back on the

European mainland – which it would not leave again for a thousand years, all the while becoming the centre of an ever-growing cult...

The power of the spear had, in fact, first been demonstrated almost 600 years earlier than the Battle of Brunanburh when the Roman emperor, Constantine the Great, used it to help Christianise his vast empire. By a curious twist of fate, this episode in the weapon's history also started in England at York – though long before it had fallen into the hands of the Vikings.

Constantine, whose real name was Flavius Valerius Aurelius Constantinus, was born at Naissus in Upper Dacia in 272. He was the eldest son of Constantius Chlorus, a soldier destined for greatness who fell in love with a woman of humble origins. Their son distinguished himself as a soldier in Diocletian's famous Expedition to Egypt in 296 and also served under Galerius in the Persian Wars.

When, in 305, the two Roman emperors, Diocletian and Maximum abdicated and Galerius and Constantine Chlorus took over as Caesari, the younger Constantine joined his father who ruled the western half of the empire from Boulogne. That year, father and son crossed the Channel in an expedition against the Picts. The older Constantine died at Eboracum, later the city of York. He had always intended his son to be his successor, and his loyal troops lost no time in proclaiming the young Constantine as their emperor on 25 July. Aware of his popularity and military skills, Galerius did not question the decision, though he granted him only the title of Caesar.

During the next eighteen years, Constantine found himself embroiled in one political controversy after another, with no less than six emperors struggling for supremacy in the empire. There was also a series of wars in which the great soldier battled his rivals for absolute power, culminating in his crossing the Alps via Mont Cenis and marching on Rome. There, on the outskirts of the city on the Milvian Bridge, he met his destiny.

Rumour and legend has made much of this action in which the emperor Maxentius was defeated and fell from the bridge and drowned. Some reports have claimed that Constantine had a vision of a 'flaming cross' before the battle which inspired him to great bravery; others that he 'carried before him a holy spear' to rouse his men. Certainly, this is the version recorded by Eusebius of Caesarea (c. 264–340), 'The Father of Christian History' in his *Life of Constantine*, which records how the emperor was convinced, 'that he needed some more powerful aid than his military forces could afford him on account of the wicked and magical enchantments which were so diligently practised by his enemies'. Eusebius even provides a description of the now elaborately embellished spear:

It was a long spear, overlaid with gold. On the top was fixed a wreath of gold and precious stones, and within this the symbol of the Saviour's name, two letters indicating the name of Christ by means of its initial characters – those letters the emperor was in the habit of wearing on his helmet at a later period. From the spear was also suspended a cloth, a royal piece, covered with a profuse embroidery of most brilliant precious stones and which, being also richly interlaced with gold, presented an indescribable degree of beauty to the beholder. The emperor constantly made use of this sign of salvation as a safeguard against every adverse and hostile power, and commanded that it should be carried at the head of all his armies.

Constantine emerged from the carnage on the Milvian Bridge a changed man. The spear, he believed, had aided his victory and its power was evidently greater than any of the pagan gods he had previously worshipped. In that moment he was converted to Christianity and vowed to Christianise the Roman Empire of which he was now the sole master.

Good as his word, Constantine legalised Christianity, alt-ough he made no attempt to have it declared the state religion or to outlaw paganism. He also devoted himself to the correction of abuses, the strengthening of his frontiers and containing the barbarian hordes that roamed across Europe.

In 325, Constantine called the first Church Council of Nicaea to settle a number of public schisms, including a dispute about the person and godhead of

Jesus. A report of the gathering says that while the arguments raged around the emperor he sat quietly on a dais, 'grasping the holy talisman of power and revelation to his breast'.

Once his authority had been established throughout the Roman Empire, Constantine rebuilt the ancient Greek city of Byzantium, naming it Nova Roma, and providing offices and a Senate similar to those in Rome. He is said to have played an important part in the reconstruction, carrying the spear around with him as if for inspiration while the boundaries of properties and open spaces for the public were settled. As he walked about, he repeated loudly enough for all to hear, 'I follow in the steps of Him whom I see walking ahead of me.' (After his death in May 337, the city was renamed Constantinople, 'City of Constantine', and later became the capital of the empire.)

The great man's final years were marked by major victories against the Vandals, the Marcomani and the Visigoths, encouraging him to plan the conquest of Persia – something no Roman emperor had contemplated since Trajan. At home, though, his rule was stained by bloodshed: in particular by the execution of his eldest son, Crispus, in 326 for treason, and his second wife, Fausta, the following year, on a similar charge.

Constantine the Great – whose epithet was given him long after his death by Christian historians – was succeeded by his three sons, Constantine II, Constantius II and Constans who secured their hold on the empire by murdering a number of their father's relatives and supporters. They presided over the dissolution of a great empire with scarcely a regret among them.

The last member of Constantine's dynasty was his grandson, Julian, who is said to have ridiculed the stories of the holy lance and tried to restore paganism in place of Christianity throughout the empire. However, just as Constantine's great success had been ascribed to the power of the spear, so Julian's failure was attributed to its invincibility.

The Emperor Julian's scepticism about the spear was not shared by his successors who continued to use its powers to inspire the Roman cause, to galvanise its troops to conquer new territories, and to convert heathens to Christianity. Emperor Theodosius (347–395) who was also to be given the nomenclature 'Great', removed the last vestiges of paganism with the aid of the spear. Indeed its likeness was imprinted on the authority of the prefects who were sent to Egypt, Syria and Asia Minor in 388 to destroy pagan temples and break up infidel associations. Throughout the empire, all pagan sacrifices, prophesying and witchcraft became punishable by law.

Theodosius was born at Cauca in northwest Spain, the son of a Roman general. He took up soldiering in his youth and won fame by his exploits in Moesia and Thrace. However, after an intrigue brought about the disgrace and execution of his father, Theodosius retired to live in his native Spain. His reputation was not forgotten, however, and he was soon called back to arms by Gracian to rule the Empire jointly with him and help subdue the Goths who were then pillaging the countryside at will. Theodosius not only subdued the vast pagan army, but was also able to recruit many of its men to his ranks and his religion.

Like his predecessor, Theodosius conducted a meeting of the Church Council at Constantinople in 381 with the spear visible at his side. When his empire was threatened some four years later by an army of barbarians, led by Arbogast and Eugenius, he led his men into battle wielding the holy relic above his head. Although initially beaten back, Theodosius refused to retreat and attacked again the following day shouting the battle cry, 'Where is the God of Theodosius?'

This time, his cry was answered, and there was no stopping the Emperor's impetus. By nightfall he had slain both Arbogast and Eugenius and left their bodies on the battlefield. In thanks for this victory, Theodosius placed the spear on display in the cathedral of Milan for a year where it attracted thousands of curious viewers.

The spear next passed into the hands of Alaric (c. 370–410), a Visigoth king who had been converted to Christianity by Theodosius and recruited into his service. Following the emperor's death in 395, the auxiliaries rebelled against the rule of Rome and chose Alaric as their leader. A ferocious fighter and natural leader, he wasted no time in invading Thrace, Macedonia and Greece. However, he was driven out of

Peloponnesus by the Roman General Stilicho and settled for a time with his hordes in Epirus. Here he conceived a daring plan to invade Italy and take Rome.

After a series of indecisive battles with the Roman legions – and several attempts by the authorities in Rome to negotiate a peaceful settlement, all of which were dishonoured – Alaric and his men finally stormed into the city. As they careered through the streets, the Goths ransacked private houses and public buildings, seizing all the gold, silver and valuables they could lay their hands on.

Alaric's prize haul, says the Byzantine historian Procopius of Caesarea who accompanied General Belisarius in his campaigns against the Goths in Italy in 536, was a familiar item, as he explained in his *Historiae* written in 562:

In the midst of the pillage, Alaric dressed himself in splendid robes and sat upon the throne of the emperor with a golden crown upon his head and the holy spear that pierced Christ in his hand. While Alaric sat upon the throne, thousands of Romans were compelled to kneel down on the ground before him and shout out his name as conqueror and emperor. After six days of pillage and pleasure, Alaric and his army marched through the gates carrying with them the riches of Rome.

It is not clear whether Alaric took the spear with him

when he left the city – but his days were already numbered. He marched south to attack Sicily and Africa, but while his fleet was at sea it was struck by a terrible storm and most of the vessels were wrecked. Alaric was one of the lucky ones to survive and managed to sail back to the mainland.

However, Alaric was already ill from his ordeal and soon afterwards died at Cosenza. Legend says that in order to hide the body and the treasure that had been seized from the Romans, the surviving members of his coterie buried both a considerable distance to the north in the bed of the Bussento River, which they had temporarily diverted from its course. The Roman slaves who had been employed to dig this burial place were then put to death in order to ensure its secrecy.

For some years afterwards there were rumours about this. But the reappearance of the spear only a quarter of a century later in the possession of Aetius, a Roman general, seems to disprove this claim.

Aetius (c. 390–454) is often referred to in the history books as the 'Last of the Romans' for his part in maintaining the empire against the barbarians. Born at Dorostolus in Moesia, the son of Gaudentius, who may well have been a barbarian, Aetius rose spectacularly in the service of Rome and was later given an honorary post in Africa He spent some years among the Goths – including a period as a hostage of Alaric – and later with Rhuas, King of the Huns, where he picked up considerable knowledge of their ways that would later prove invaluable to him when he changed sides.

In 425, Aetius was at the head of over 60,000 barbarians who had allied with Rome against her enemies, a move which enhanced his own position in the hierarchy and made him *Magister Militumper Gallas* (Master of Soldiers in Gaul). From 433 to 451 he was undoubtedly one of the most dominating characters in the Roman world and was responsible for putting down a revolt against the empire by Count Boniface.

Contemporary accounts of this action speak of Aetius fatally wounding Boniface with 'a javelin', However, some chroniclers believe the word should be translated as 'spear' and as a result this incident may well represent the first use of the holy relic as an actual weapon since it had belonged to the Roman centurion.

Aetius did much to sustain the declining status of the Roman Empire at this time and achieved his greatest victory at the Battle of Chalon – the modern Chalons-en-Champagne – on 20 September 451 when he defeated forces led by the infamous Attila the Hun. Once again there are stories of him brandishing the spear as he charged into battle and later proudly displaying it to his triumphant troops at the end of the bloody fight.

The Battle of Chalons was to prove Aetius' last great triumph, however. Three years later, he visited the Emperor Valentinian III to seek permission for his son, Gaudentius, to marry the ruler's daughter. Resentful of the general's success and suspecting he might have ambitions for the throne himself, Valentinian brutally stabbed him to death.

There is a curious footnote to this account. According to some reports, Attila (*c.* 406–453), the 'Scourge of God', briefly gained possession of the spear during the time he was cutting his swathe of destruction across Europe, following his accession as King of the Huns in 434. His many conquests finally came to a halt almost twenty years later in Italy in 452 after he had devastated Aquileia, Milan, Padua and reached the very gates of Rome. There, it is said, he was bought off from sacking the city by the intervention of Pope Leo I with the offer of a vast treasure trove – an offer he may well have been glad to accept in order not to have to put his army, weakened by famine and pestilence, to yet another test.

The story says that just before he headed north, Attila galloped his horse back to the gates of Rome. Pausing, he drew what looked like a slim weapon from his saddle and hurled it in the direction of a group of officers waiting nervously to see if he would keep his word to depart. Rearing his horse before riding off, the fearsome warrior shouted: 'Take back your holy lance – it is no use to me since I do not know Him that made it holy'.

There, in the dust at the men's feet, lay the Spear of Longinus.

Whatever the truth of the story of Attila, the holy lance is next recorded during the reign of Emperor Justinian

I (*c.* 482–565), who was famous for codifying the Roman constitutions and statues known as the *Codex Justinianus* and *Novellae Constitutiones*. These influential decrees were no mean achievement for a man born Petrus Sabbatius, the son of a Slavonic peasant, in the small village of Tauresina on the Balkan Peninsula.

Justinian's mother, Vigilanta, was the sister of General Justin, who adopted the child as his son and saw him properly educated at Constantinople. Although the boy initially studied law and philosophy, it was military matters that really excited his interest and he advanced rapidly in the Roman army – no doubt helped by the patronage of his stepfather.

In 521 Justinian became a consul and soon after was made regent. Six years later he achieved the ultimate accolade when he was proclaimed Emperor. He also broke new ground in Roman tradition by marrying an actress, Theodora, in 523. At the time, such women were considered little better than prostitutes – yet their union which proved extremely happy demonstrated Justinian's commendable determination to break down social barriers.

The new emperor was also intent on restoring the Roman Empire to its former glory and went to war on several fronts, successfully reconquering North Africa, Sicily, Northern Italy and Spain. He also extended a vast line of fortifications along the eastern and south eastern frontier of his territories.

Though Justinian was undeniably a man of great

purpose and energy, he was also unscrupulous and crafty, according to his biographer, Procopius, in *Historia Arcana*. The emperor had no qualms about using the most savage methods when imposing the rule of Rome – quashing a rebellion in one pagan corner of the empire with the slaughter of 35,000 people. These actions were carried out in the name of Christianity and a number of groups whose beliefs did not match his own - notably the Jews and the Greeks – were persecuted by him.

Procopius tells us that apart from Justinian's interests in jurisprudence and philosophy, he was also very intrigued by the legend of the holy spear. He was convinced that possessing it ensured his destiny. It was one of the most revered of his possessions – the Byzantine historian writes – and was once publicly used to explain his decision to abolish the Academy of Plato in Athens: 'He declared upon the Holy Spear that it was his task to suppress Hellenism and all forms of paganism.'

This decision – and the savagery of some of his military actions – left Justinian's critics feeling that such extremism ill-matched the symbol of the Messiah. Indeed, his rule was to be followed by a period of 200 years when nothing was heard of the spear and even its existence began to be questioned.

All this would change, however, in the reign of the legendary Charlemagne when a dramatic new chapter in its history would begin. Then, too, the spear's origins would also be thrown open to doubt...

Five

'The Lance of the Lord'

Charlemagne – or, in English, Charles the Great – was King of the Franks, Emperor of the West and one of the greatest rulers in history. A man of commanding presence, enormous courage and possessing a great tactical sense, he fought almost fifty campaigns and carved his name indelibly into the late eighth and early ninth century, earning a reputation that has become synonymous with great civilising powers exemplified in heroic legends and romances.

He is also believed by some authorities to have been the man who was responsible for creating the holy spear that has travelled down the ages and now resides in Vienna.

The life and career of Charlemagne has, of course, been recounted in a constant flow of biographies, so a precis here will surely surface. He was born in Aachen in 742, the son of Pepin the Short, King of the Franks. After his father's death in 768, Charles inherited the northern part of the kingdom, while his younger brother, Carloman, was left to rule the remainder.

Within three years, however, Carloma had died and Charles took possession of the entire Frankish kingdom. His legend – and that of the dynasty he founded – now began to take shape.

In 772, while Charles was engaged in the first of his many campaigns, fighting and Christianising the pagan Saxons, he received a request from Pope Adrian I for help against the equally troublesome Lombards. He at once set out with his men across the Alps and in 773 captured Pavia, assumed the title of King of the Lombards and gave Ravenna to the papal see. In the years that followed he was kept busy with suppressing an insurrection in Italy, making the Westphalian leader, Widukind, submit to his rule, and finally pacifying all the Saxon factions.

The year 777 saw Charles receive another call for help – this time from the emir of Saragossa who was being besieged by the emir of Cordova. Once again he took the direct route to the scene of the conflict, crossing the Pyrenées and reached the River Ebro. The rearguard action at Roncesvalles in which Roland, warden of the Breton March, and other Frankish nobles were ambushed and slaughtered by Basque hordes, later became immortalised in the *Chanson de Roland*.

By now, tales of the feats of the mighty Frankish King were spreading across Europe as he absorbed Bavaria and the lands of the Avars in Hungary into his domains, making Christians of the people in the process. In 800 he marched into Italy to support Pope Leo III, crushing

5 Charlegmane and the holy spear portrayed on a coin

all who dared to stand in his way. On Christmas Day, he rode in triumph to St Peter's Church where he was crowned by the grateful pontiff as Carolus Augustus, emperor of the Romans – an action that confirmed his supremacy throughout the western world.

The list of the new emperor's achievements appeared to many people as almost superhuman – a fact that grew in the popular imagination when it was learned that he had in his possession the spear that had pierced the body of Christ. This fact is confirmed by Eginhard, a Frankish historian who became a great favourite in the emperor's court and in 820 wrote the definitive biography, *Life of Charlemagne* – a work undeniably dedicated to glorifying its subject.

In his account, Eginhard is at pains to show that the

emperor's achievements were not solely confined to conquest, although his vast empire ultimately stretched from the Ebro to the Elbe. Charlemagne had learned to speak Latin and read Greek, had revised the laws of the Franks, introduced trial by jury, reformed weights and measures and minted a new coinage. He also took a great interest in theology, organised the Church in his domains and prompted monastic reform and missionary work, inspiring what historians have since referred to as the 'Carolingian Renaissance'.

Eginhard is more specific about the role of the spear in Charlemagne's life in his *Annales Francorum*, where he writes that the Emperor 'founded his dynasty on possession of the Holy Spear and its power to control destiny'. The historian says that Charles had a great interest in the old heroic lays and encouraged scholars throughout his kingdom to collect and preserve any documents or artefacts that substantiated these tales.

According to the book, Charlemagne carried the holy spear with him on every one of his forty-seven campaigns to ensure victory. The weapon also apparently enhanced his clairvoyant powers, enabling him to discover the burial place of St James in Spain and to anticipate future events, Eginhard states, continuing:

Throughout his life, the emperor lived and slept within reach of his beloved talisman. Only when he accidentally let it fall from his hands, while returning from his final victorious campaign, did his subjects rightly see it as an augury of tragedy and his imminent death.

Elaborating on this statement, Eginhard says that while Charlemagne was returning from Saxony, a comet suddenly flashed across the sky. At this, the emperor's horse shied and threw him to the ground. The holy spear, which he had been holding in his left had, was dashed from his grasp and thrown twenty feet away from him into the dust.

'At this same moment, unbeknown to Charlemagne, there were earth tremors at the Royal Palace in Aachen. The word *Princeps* mysteriously faded from the red ochre inscription high up on a central beam which had formerly read, *Karolus Princeps*.'

Charlemagne died in Aachen, the city where he had been born, on 28 January 814 and was soon being fêted in the same kind of stories and ballads he had enjoyed as a young man. These epics by the likes of Ludovico Ariosto, Matteo Boiardo and Torquato Tasso also praised the achievements of the Carolingian Dynasty that he had founded.

There are, however, experts on ancient history who believe that Eginhard is guilty of invention and elaboration in his account of the spear. They believe that Charlemagne was obsessed with promoting his 'thousand-year empire', and ordered the making of his own replica of the lance as a deliberate counter to a

symbol used by the Merovingian Empire he had
overthrown. The insignia of the Merovingians was an
ancient 'Tribal Spear' that symbolised spiritual
leadership under the Tribal God and his power of life
and death over all the Frankish people. As a Christian,
Charlemagne held the ' Spear of Longinus' to be
symbolic of the Blood of Christ giving its owner the
power to rule by 'divine right.'

As we learned earlier, the experiments by Professor
Robert Feather in Vienna indicate the lance in Vienna
might well be no older than the time of Charlemagne.
But such a verdict, correct or not, does not solve the
secret of the Spear of Destiny – it merely enhances the
mystery surrounding it and takes us into even stranger
areas of enquiry.

It is a sad fact, as history relates, that Charlemagne's
attempt to consolidate order and Christian culture
among the nations of the West was doomed to failure.
His successors lacked his qualities of greatness and the
empire fell to pieces. However, the story of the
Emperor of the West and his holy spear gathered
momentum with the passing years, each generation
growing more convinced of its remarkable powers.
One of the first scholars to write at length about it was
an Italian prelate and historian named Liutprand, who
methodically traced its history and fervently denied any
suggestions that it might have originated in the time of
Charlemagne.

Unfortunately, not a great deal is known about the early years of this primary biographer of the spear, beyond the fact he was born around 922 of a Longobard family in Pavia and in 931 entered the service of King Hugo of Italy as a page. Evidence suggests Liutprand was an intelligent, ambitious man who loved gossip and revelled in political machinations – abilities that helped him to rise quickly in court circles. By the time King Hugo had been replaced by his successor, Berengar I, the page had become a chancellor.

In 949, Liutprand was dispatched as an ambassador to the Byzantine court in Constantinople. Here he wrote a brilliant and scathing account of court life, *Relatio de Legatione Constantinoplitana*, which is widely regarded as one of the most graphic and lively pieces of writing about the tenth century – although one which quickly offended and even outraged some of its noble readers.

On his return to Italy, Liutprand found himself in disgrace with the King and, particularly, his manipulative wife, Willa, and was forced to leave the court. He did not take long, however, to find a new position in the service of Emperor Otto I (the Great), the man who would establish his medieval German kingdom as the leading power in Western Europe. Here Liutprand's intelligence and scheming endeared him to the monarch and the two men shared many confidences. Indeed, it was Otto who aroused Liutprand's interest in the holy lance with the story of how it had been given to him as part of the dowry when he married his wife, Edith, the half-sister of Britain's King Athelstan in 939.

The life of Otto I since that date had been one of almost constant achievement – beginning with a remarkably successful campaign in Saxony where he carried the spear constantly at his side, as described by Liutprand in his book *Monumentis Germaniae Historicis Recusa*. This narrative of events in German history – and in Otto's life especially – also had a secondary purpose. It enabled its author to avenge himself on Berengar and his queen. In its pages, he lauded Otto's military genius and how he had expanded his territories, colonised whole nations and promoted Christianity eastward into the Slavic world. All in a campaign that bore many similarities to the Carolingian model of Charlemagne – which Liutprand took considerable delight in pointing out.

Otto's skill as a general was based on his unique ability to coordinate long-distance strategic movement and to keep forces from widely differing regions working together. These qualities marked the King's most important campaigns – the defeat of the Magyars at the Battle of Lechfield (near Vienna) in 955 and his earlier expedition across the Alps in 951 by which he secured control of Italy. After both of these victories he gave thanks to the 'holy spear' that had made them possible.

According to Liutprand, Otto 'shared the piety and superstition of the age and did much for the spread of

Christianity'. The king also believed that owning the spear had prevented his death at the hand of his brother, Henry of Bavaria, who resented the spread of his sibling's empire. At Christmas 941, a plot was hatched to murder Otto by sending two assassins to kill him while he was at prayer. Sensing the men approaching, the King had seized the spear from where it lay on the altar and driven both of them away. The pair were apparently soon captured by royal guards and duly executed.

Liultprand also wrote in his *Monumentis*, 'Otto quashed revolts among the warlike tribes living between the Elbe and the Oder by using the superstitions around the spear to Christianise them'. He also alluded to the age of the weapon and allied it firmly to the life of Constantine the Great, the first Christian Roman emperor.

In 951, Otto sent an ambassador to the Pope with a request that he be crowned Holy Roman emperor, as Charlemagne had been before him. 'The request was denied,' reports Liutprand, 'but although Otto had been rather presumptuous in his determined efforts to mount the imperial throne, the privileged holder of the Holy Spear of Longinus knew that it would only be a matter of time before he achieved his ultimate destiny.'

So it proved. Otto was crowned emperor in 962 by Pope John XII. A highlight of this event, according to his biographer, occurred when the king knelt before the Pope and 'was touched upon the shoulder by the lance as a holy rite to establish his claim as Holy Roman Emperor'. Liutprand's own reward for his loyalty to his master was to be made Bishop of Cremona where his light clerical duties left him free to pursue his literary endeavours.

However, the relationship between Otto and Pope John began to founder when the papacy turned against the emperor because of his burgeoning power. Once again Otto acted decisively, removing John from the papacy and imposing a rule that in future no pope would be elected without the approval of the emperor. History has shown that this proclamation opened an era of German domination of the papacy and, in effect, made Otto head of the Christian community.

According to Liutprand, Otto believed the holy lance 'represented the essence of his power'. It enabled him to maintain control throughout the once troubled states of Germany and Italy, as well as establishing Christianity in Scandinavia and the Slavonic lands. Equally, it symbolised his own supreme authority and was kept under constant guard on a podium in the opulent cathedral he built in Magdeburg in 968. It was here that he was buried following his death in 973.

Liutprand, the king's devoted chronicler, had died the previous year and with his passing references to the spear were to be scant for almost a century. When it did emerge again into the public eye, however, two startling new additions had been made to the blade.

*

The reign of Henry IV, the third German Holy Roman emperor, was categorised by his attempts to consolidate imperial power and a number of clashes with the Church. Notwithstanding these, his name is indelibly associated with the legend of the spear because of the restoration and additions he ordered to be made to the increasingly fragile relic.

Born in Goslar, Henry was only six years old when his father, the campaigning Henry III, died. Initially, his mother, the empress Agnes, ruled on his behalf until 1070, after which he began to act for himself. His first task was to break the power of the Saxon nobles – but his drastic and bloody measures to achieve this provoked an uprising that overwhelmed his forces in 1074. The following year, according to a study of his life by the historian, Friedrich Floto, written in 1855, Henry armed himself with 'the spear of Christ' and defeated his foes at Hohenburg.

But the King's troubles were actually only just beginning. In 1075, trying to maintain the loyalty of his people and the support of the Pope, he jeopardised both by insisting on the right of the ruler to appoint members of the clergy, in particular the bishops. This decision began the conflict known as the 'Investiture Controversy', which resulted in Henry being excommunicated by Pope Gregory VII in February 1076. Sensing that he was losing the support of both sides, the King begged the Pope to rescind the sentence. The Pontiff agreed – but only after Henry had showed his repentance by walking barefoot from his court at Canossa to Rome.

Sore in mind and body, the king vowed to have revenge. Soon he was busy plotting once more to overthrow the pope and again found himself excommunicated. This time there would be no pleading for mercy. In 1084 he stormed across the Alps with a large army, lay siege to Rome, and after the city had fallen proclaimed himself emperor.

To mark his coronation, Henry ordered the holy spear to be brought to Rome. According to Floto, he summoned the finest jeweller in Italy and instructed him to make two additions to the relic. The first was to integrate a 'holy nail' into the blade that he said had come from the cross on which Christ had been crucified. The other was to encircle it with a silver band bearing the inscription: *Clavus Dominicos* – 'Nail of Our Lord'.

The reappearance of the restored spear at Henry's coronation created a sensation. News of the addition of the crucifixion nail also spread like wildfire across Europe, fanned by Henry's claim that the lance's power had been redoubled, making the authority of its owner even more secure He made no attempt to justify the provenance of the nail, however.

Whether this tinkering with the lance affected its power or not, there is no doubt that the remainder of Henry' s reign was very unsettled. In his absence from Germany, three rivals for his throne had arisen, although on his return he was able to overpower them all. Then one of his sons, Conrad, challenged his authority, only to be followed by a second offspring, Henry – the latter taking his father prisoner and forcing him to abdicate. Luckily, the old man was able to escape from a bloody end and fled speedily to safety in Liège where he died, deeply disheartened, on 7 August 1106.

Among the last acts of this troubled man – so one version of the legend records – was to give the spear secretly into the keeping of his beloved daughter, Agnes, who had all the time remained faithful to him. In her hands it was to pass into the vastly influential Hohenstaufen family as a result of her marriage to its greatest scion, Frederick I, named Barbarossa, or 'Red-Beard', after his long and impressive auburn beard.

There were few greater medieval emperors than Frederick I, a tall, majestic looking man who was so loved by his people that it was said, 'Germany and Frederick Barbarossa are one in the hearts of the Germans'. Indeed, a legend grew up after his death that he had not died, but was asleep with a group of his knights in the Kyffhauser Mountain in Saxony waiting to be summoned. 'When the ravens cease to fly around the mountain,' the story says, 'Barbarossa will awake and restore Germany to its ancient greatness.'

Some versions of this legend claim that the holy spear, which aided all Frederick's actions, is still clutched in his right hand, although others believe it is his great two-handed sword. In any event, the legend was to have a

profound effect on many generations of Germans – not
the least of them Adolf Hitler who idolised the man and
called his hideaway in the Ober Salzburg mountains,
'Barbarossa' and gave the code-name, 'Operation
Barbarossa,' to his invasion of Russia in 1941.

Frederick was born in 1125, the son of Frederick of
Hohenstaufen, Duke of Swabia, and his wife, Judith of
Bavaria, of the rival Guelph dynasty. The fact that the
boy was descended from Germany's two principal
families made him an acceptable choice as heir to the
throne. He was just twenty-five when he succeeded his
father – and five years later, on 4 March 1152, he
became the Holy Roman emperor in place of his
uncle, Conrad III.

Barbarossa's life was to prove one long unyielding
struggle with problems at home, civic unrest in
Lombardy and disputes with the Pope in Rome. He
undertook six expeditions to Italy, during which his
relations with the Pope Adrian IV gradually
deteriorated, culminating in 1076 with a bloody battle
and his defeat at the Battle of Legnano. This, however,
proved to be more valuable to him that his previous
successes, for it changed his previous uncompromising
policy to one of clemency and concession, which
finally resulted in the Lombards becoming peaceful
citizens.

In 1177, he acknowledged the papacy of Alexander III
at a ceremony where the holy spear was displayed to the
assembled multitudes. According to a contemporary

document, 'At Venice, Frederick Red-Beard knelt with the spear in his hands and kissed the feet of the Pope he had once defeated.'

To fulfil his great ambition of making Germany a united nation demanded all Frederick's military skill, his unbounded energy and courage, not to mention his supreme ability as an administrator. He was also called upon to demonstrate a ruthless streak in order to frighten and charm people at the same time. Similarly there was the little matter of keeping the nobles in the different provinces at peace with one another, while persuading them to work together for the good of the entire empire.

During this reformation, the holy spear would often be present on the table before the fearsome red-bearded man while he passed judgement. It also went with him when he led the Third Crusade against Saladin in 1187 – an event, it is claimed, that marked the first return of the spear to the place where it had become holy over a thousand years earlier.

The Moslems had once again risen up and taken Jerusalem after it had been in Christian hands for almost ninety years. At this news, 'Red-Beard' speedily raised an army of over 150,000 men from the German Empire and set out for Palestine – accompanied by two other great Christian kings, Philip Augustus of France and Richard I of England. Once in Asia Minor, the Crusaders attacked the infidel force and defeated them after two great battles at Philomelium and Iconium.

Misfortune lay waiting for the great warrior,

however. One day, as his army was about to cross a small bridge over the River Saleph in Cilicia, he galloped up and, impatient to get over the river and join his son who was leading the advance guard, plunged his horse straight into the water. The current was stronger than he had realised, and mount and rider were immediately swept away. Frederick's heavy armour left him helpless and he drowned before assistance could reach him.

A contemporary report of the accident states, 'As he was crossing the stream, the holy spear fell from his hands at the very moment of his death. His body was recovered and buried at St Peter's in Antioch.'

No mention is to be found in this account – or any other written at the time – about the immediate fate of the spear. In fact, it would not surface again until the fourteenth century, fragile once more and now minus its wooden shaft.

Although the holy lance was not seen in public until the reign of Charles IV, the legend itself was far from forgotten. At the beginning of the thirteenth century its remarkable powers and enduring history were celebrated in one of the great epic poems of the Middle Ages, *Parsifal* by the German, Wolfram von Eschenbach, which, in its turn, would inspire one of Richard Wagner's finest librettos.

Parsifal has, of course, become one of the jewels of German literature and music, and one hundred years after its publication, Charles IV of Bohemia sought to find a similar adornment and add lustre to his rather mediocre court. Charles was the son of John of Luxemburg, the extraordinary blind King of Bohemia. Despite losing his sight in his early forties, the older man had still conducted a vigorous campaign of conquest in Austria and Italy, before falling at the Battle of Crécy on 26 August 1346 while fighting alongside the French against the English King, Edward III.

Charles was elected king of Bohemia after the death of his father and immediately began adding to his kingdom. Within a year, all Germany was under his control and he then set about fulfilling his ambition to preside over the finest centre of art and literature in Europe. In 1348 he despatched courtiers across his kingdom to find precious artefacts and rare documents for his collection. He also encouraged them to go further afield in the hope of discovering holy relics that would illuminate both his faith and his kingship.

According to a monograph on his life by Sir W. Stirling-Maxwell, Charles found exactly what he was looking for in Austria. 'In a Cistercian monastery in the Tyrol Mountains, his men discovered an ancient spearhead. Under threat, the monks reluctantly admitted that was the self-same weapon with which the Centurion at Calvary had pierced the side of Christ in His dying moments. The men hurried back with their prize to the delighted king.'

There are no clues in Stirling-Maxwell's account as to how precisely the spear had ended up in the Tyrol.

But Charles seemed happy to accept its authenticity, citing the crucifixion nail and silver band that Henry IV had added for his coronation as proof. He decided to strengthen the delicate relic by adding a new, golden sleeve over the old silver one, now tarnished by age. He also gave instructions that the inscription was to be altered to a more specific statement, 'Lance and Nail of the Lord', before it was put on display in Prague.

The Bohemian king was not merely content with possessing the spear, says Stirling-Maxwell:

He sent emissaries to the pope about his discovery. He urged the pontiff to declare an annual Feast of Longinus and commissioned a new liturgy and mass to commemorate the day. The pope gave his assent and the lance again became the centre-piece of a royal court.

Though there can be no doubt that Charles IV was the first to name the spear, 'The Lance of the Lord', there were others who were suspicious of its authenticity after it had been missing for so long. One historian, Volker Schier, has argued that the reason why the king was so anxious to have the lance verified was to show a tangible justification for his accession to the throne of all Germany.

'The prime justification seemed to have been the holy lance,' he wrote. 'Or at least he turned it into that, as it didn't have that meaning when he became king.'

True or not, the ancient spear was now on view once

again and would remain so for 500 years. In total – it is claimed – the relic would be owned by forty-five kings and emperors after Charlemagne as the years rolled by to the twentieth century. With the passing of time it was confirmed, too, as a symbol of destiny: inspiring great ambitions, affecting the fate of nations, and growing in mystique as it passed from one royal hand to the next. It became, in a sentence, a talisman of supreme power.

The next significant event in the history of the 'Lance of the Lord' occurred in the fifteenth century when it was passed to Charles' descendant, Sigismund (1368–1437), a man who lacked some of his forebear's military skills, but nevertheless possessed all his ambition and cunning. In 1396 he was heavily defeated by the Turkish army at Nicopolis, but retaliated later with a larger force and went on to conquer Bosnia, Herzegovina and Serbia. In 1411 he was made Holy Roman emperor and induced Pope John XXIII to summon the Council of Constance, ostensibly to end the schism with the Bohemian reformer John Huss. However, the king made no effort to enforce the safe conduct granted to Huss to attend the gathering, and on his journey the hapless man was seized by assassins and burned alive.

Sigismund's paranoia that he, too, might suffer such a fate – perhaps at the hands of Huss's supports who vehemently opposed his succession to the throne of Bohemia – also caused him to fear for the security of the holy spear. In 1424, he announced: 'It is the Will of God that the Imperial Crown, Orb, Sceptre, Crosses, Sword and Lance of the Holy Roman Empire must never leave the soil of the Fatherland.' To ensure this, he proposed to pass the collection of relics, collectively known as the *Reichkleinodien*, 'Imperial Regalia', to the town council of Nuremberg – for a price, of course.

The removal of the royal treasures from Prague to the German city was carried out in an operation that combined audacity with daring – they were hidden under a pile of fish in a simple wagon accompanied by just four men. The relics reached Nuremberg safely, however, and were taken to the Hospital of the Holy Ghost. There a wooden cabinet embossed with silver was made for the spear in order to hang it from the rafters of the church safe from the reach of avaricious hands.

There the spearhead remained for all to see, albeit from a height. Once a year it was taken down and displayed on the altar for the benefit of pilgrims. Among these devout souls, a legend grew up that if the lance were looked at through mirrors, those who saw it would be able to capture its 'image' and take it home. Also on display were a number of other relics including a tooth of John the Baptist, an arm bone of St Anne, and what was claimed to be a piece of wood from the manger in which the infant Jesus had slept.

Such was the fame of the spear by now that the good and the great from all over Europe came to bask in its magnetism. Isabella of Spain, for example, had an emissary bring a piece of muslin to be pierced by the point of the spear in the hope of making this a holy relic in its own right. Count Ferdinand of Austria also sent one of his courtiers with a suitably generous gift to the council for permission to have the weapon dipped in a keg of his wine – convinced that by drinking the contents he would be endowed with some of the spear's powers of invincibility.

The relic continued to remain in its skylight eerie until the army of Napoleon Bonaparte sweeping all before it across Europe, approached Nuremberg in the spring of 1796. Rumours abounded that the all-conquering Corsican intended to claim the lance as spoils of war after the Battle of Austerlitz and use it as a symbol of his power and destiny. Fearful of this happening, the city councillors decided to remove the *Reichkleinodien* to Vienna for safekeeping.

The mission was entrusted to one Baron von Hugel, an imperial envoy from Regensberg. He wasted no time in taking the precious artefacts across the border, promising that he would return them when peace had been restored. Instead, when the Holy Roman Empire was dissolved in 1806, he took advantage of the confusion over who now owned the collection and sold the regalia including the spear to the Habsburgs, the Austrian imperial family who had ruled uninterruptedly since 1440.

This crime did not, however, come to light until after

Napoleon's defeat at Waterloo. When the councillors of Nuremberg petitioned for the return of their treasures, the Austrian authorities' in Vienna summarily rejected the request. Possession of the spear and the other items was felt to be theirs by right – not to mention the right of possession and superior strength.

There, indeed, the 'Lance of the Lord' might well have remained undisturbed with the rest of the items alongside the crown jewels of the Habsburgs if it had not been seen by a curious young man with dreams of creating his own 'thousand year empire' like his hero, Charlemagne. His name was Adolf Schicklgruber – and the world would very soon get to know him far better as Adolf Hitler...

Six

Hitler and the
Magic Talisman

Room 11 of the Schatzkammer tucked away in a
courtyard of the Kunsthistorisches Museum was
deserted except for a solitary attendant, sitting rather
disinterestedly near the door, when the dishevelled
young man walked in. It was not long to closing time in
this section of the museum devoted to 'Secular and
Sacred Treasures' in the magnificent former Imperial
Palace of Vienna. The man glanced across at a clock on
the wall as the solitary visitor passed him by and began
to look at the exhibits. By the state of the visitor's
threadbare black coat, the attendant guessed he was
probably killing time on a chilly autumn afternoon
before going home to his lodgings.

The visitor, in his early twenties, had in fact been in
the Hofburg for quite a lot of the day. He had spent
time in Room 1 with its insignia, staffs of office and
documents relating to the running of the Austrian
Archduchies, followed by an hour in Room 5 with its
memorabilia of Napoleon. He had briefly looked into
Room 7 which displayed jewellery and gemstones,

before moving on to the heirlooms of the long-ruling Habsburg family in Room 8. Here he studied the strange 'Horn of the Unicorn' and then turned to an extraordinary agate bowl with a pattern that was said to spell out the name of Christ.

The young man read the notices in German below the two items. The unicorn, it said, was a fabled beast of the Middle Ages, believed to symbolise the Virgin Birth and the incarnation of Jesus Christ. Miraculous powers had been attributed to its horn and examples had been sold for vast fortunes. However, this particular eight-foot (2.4m) long 'horn', had been identified as the tusk of a narwhal dating from the sixteenth century and had been a gift from King Sigismund to Ferdinand I in 1540.

The bowl was even more intriguing. For many years it had been revered as the 'Holy Grail' in which the blood of Christ on the Cross had been collected. It had apparently been obtained in Constantinople in 1204 during the Fourth Crusade and found its way into the Habsburg collection by way of their predecessors, the Babenbergs. An image of the bowl remained in the young man's mind as he walked on through the museum with thoughts of its religious significance flitting through his imagination, despite the fact he had not been a churchgoer for years.

In another of the Schatzkammer's room he had the opportunity of examining some of the museum's more dubious relics. In one glass-fronted display case was what was said to be a wooden fragment of the 'True

1. A twelfth-century Greek illustration of Longinus at the
Crucifixion. Christ's blood is being caught in the Holy Grail

2. A copy made in 1606 of the holy spear in the Ciborium at St Peter's basilica in Rome

3. Charlemagne with the holy lance – a picture by the French artist Vétault

4. The spear being carried by the Crusader Count Raymond in June 1098

5. A nineteenth-century sketch of 'The Lance of St Maurice'

6. Hitler – The Ice Lover – who planned to use the spear to rule the world

7. The holy lance with other items of the Holy Roman Empire treasures in Vienna

8. Dr Walter Stein who traced the history of Adolf Hitler
and the holy spear

10. The most recent photograph of the elusive holy spear of Armenia

9. The Cracow spear in Poland that is believed to be one of several copies

11. Gheghardavank – The Monastery of the Holy Lance

Cross' lying alongside a jewelled seventeenth-century artefact from Augsburg containing a nail claimed to have been prised from the cross. Nearby was a shred of the tablecloth from the Last Supper and one of St Peter's teeth that had been presented to Emperor Franz Joseph by the pope in 1853 after the young emperor had narrowly escaped assassination.

The young visitor was beginning to feel a bit weary when he finally entered Room 11. At first glance it contained more ornate regalia – a number of orbs, sceptres, crowns and swords, each resting on red plush cushions. His eyes fell on the 'Sabre of Charlemagne' and a Carolingian book of the gospels on which the great king's successors had sworn their oaths. More impressive still was the octagonal crown of the Holy Roman emperor that dated from the tenth century. Encrusted with gems and pearls, set with enamel plaques and surmounted by a cross rising above the brow-plate, it had been made by a German goldsmith for the coronation of Otto the Great in 962, a notice below stated. The card added that the regalia had come into the Habsburg's possession in 1440 – when Friedrich III had been crowned the last Holy Roman emperor – and had been sequestered for a time in 1806 by the French emperor Napoleon.

Just as the dishevelled figure was about to turn away, another exhibit stopped him in his tracks. Nowhere near as grand or bedecked with precious stones as the other relics, there was still something curiously

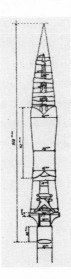

6 Illustration from the Schatkammer catalogue, c.1910

fascinating about the little object resting on the bottom
of the display case. He looked closer. It was an iron
spearhead, blackened with age, circled with gold and
silver bands and with a nail in the centre of the blade.
The printed card beside it said simply *Heilige Lanze,
Karolingisch, c. 8Jh.*

How long the visitor stood lost in reverie until he
heard the bell being sounded for the closing of the
museum he was not sure. But the impact of seeing this
unprepossessing object would inspire him for the rest of
his life, according to his own version of the event:

I knew with immediacy that this was an important
moment in my life and yet I could not divine why an

outwardly Christian symbol should make such an impression upon me. I stood there quietly gazing upon it quite oblivious to the scene of the Schatzkammer around me. It seemed to carry some hidden inner meaning which evaded me, a meaning which I felt I inwardly knew, yet could not bring to consciousness.

When the young man *did* learn the full story of the spearhead, it would indeed profoundly affect his life and very nearly change the destiny of the whole world.

The young visitor to the Hofburg on that winter day in 1912 was Adolf Schicklgruber, née Hitler, just twenty-three years old, a struggling artist with few prospects and a huge chip on his shoulder. His life to that moment had been one long chapter of frustration and failure – although his birth date of 20 April 1889 in Braunau-am-Inn, Austria seemed heavy with significance because the same date in 753 was by tradition the date of the foundation of Rome.

Intended by his father who was a customs official, for the civil service, the young Adolf instead saw himself as a great artist. This ambition may, indeed, have been the reason he deliberately did badly in his school leaving examinations. After his father's death, he attended a private art school in Munich, but failed twice to gain admission to the Vienna Academy of Arts. Advised to try architecture instead, he was again debarred because of his lack of a leaving certificate. His rabid hatred of intellectuals and his later sneers at the 'gentlemen with diplomas' – not to mention his anti-Semitic views – all evidently originated at this period of his life.

From 1904 to 1913, Hitler scraped a living in Vienna by selling postcard sketches and doing the occasional spot of interior decorating. He also became fascinated with the occult, buying those books on the subject he could afford from second-hand dealers and reading the rest in the city's public libraries. According to historian Alan Bullock in his classic work, *Hitler – A Study in Tyranny* (1952), his reading was 'wide-ranging and often indiscriminate from Ancient Rome to the Eastern Religions, Yoga, Occultism, Hypnotism and Astrology'.

Undoubtedly, the time Hitler spent in the ancient city was to have a profound affect on his future as he later admitted in his book *Mein Kampf*:

Vienna was and remained for me the hardest, though most thorough, school of my life. In this period there took shape within me the world picture and philosophy which became the granite foundation of all my acts. In addition to what I then created, I have had to learn little; and I have had to alter nothing.

The outbreak of the First World War, however, was to provide the young drifter with his first chance to prove himself. In 1914, Hitler enrolled in the 16th Bavarian Reserve Infantry Regiment and after a short period of training was sent to the front line at Ypres. Here he survived a terrible baptism of fire that claimed the lives of 3,000 men in his regiment. Hitler himself displayed considerable bravery and was awarded an Iron Cross, Second Class.

For much of the rest of the conflict, Hitler served as a Meld ganger, or military runner, carrying messages between headquarters and the units at the front. Here again he showed such courage and dedication to duty – including, it is claimed, single-handedly capturing a French officer and fifteen men – that he was made a corporal and then in August 1918 awarded an Iron Cross, First Class.

Adolf Hitler's blaze of glory was, however, cut short when he was caught in a British mustard gas attack. He was still lying wounded in hospital when Germany surrendered – the shock even more painful and traumatic than the wounds he was suffering. He returned to Munich in November 1918, where his wartime achievements were recognised by the *Reichswehr* (military authorities) and he was assigned to the Intelligence Branch to spy on the activities of small political parties, as Nigel Pennick has described in *Hitler's Secret Sciences* (1981):

Before long, he had infiltrated the ranks of several occult-political groups which the authorities thought subversive One day, his masters sent him along to a beer hall where a new group was holding a meeting. It was called the German Workers' party, and any party

with the word 'Worker' in its title was naturally
suspected of being anarchist or communist. Hitler
soon found out otherwise and joined as member
number 7. He was soon to impose his own creed on
the party, naming it at the same time the National
Socialist German Workers' Party, Nazi for short.

The strange origins of the party also had a special
appeal for Hitler. Unlike most extremist groups, he
found it was more mystical than political and its
members interested in the same things that he was.
There was a heavy emphasis on mystical symbolism and
Hitler had become increasingly interested in the
magical theory behind regalia ever since his visit to
Room 11 in the Vienna museum.

He felt there was a deeper magic behind certain relics
and artefacts. He sensed that the magic inherent in these
symbols could be transferred to a new owner and by
possessing – even confiscating them – the power could
be his. Ownership would be more than just symbolic, it
would have an actual, functioning reality that could
shape his own destiny and that of the new German
world he was so desperately keen to see...

The revelation of Hitler's obsession with the occult and
particularly 'Die Heilige Lanze ' as a result of his first
sight of it in the Schatzkammer museum is generally
credited to the English writer, Trevor Ravenscroft, and
his book, *The Spear of Destiny*, first published in London

in 1972. In fact, though, the story had actually first been exposed more than twelve years earlier in a remarkable piece of investigative journalism by a peripatetic Irish writer named Max Caulfield – whose work, curiously, Ravenscroft does not mention in his text, acknowledgements or even bibliography.

It is difficult to believe that as both men spoke to the same source during the course of their enquiries that Ravenscroft was not aware of Caulfield's earlier research. Be that as it may – and the reader can draw his own conclusions about this omission – I propose to give credit where credit is due and consider the life and work of Caulfield first and return to Ravenscroft in the next chapter.

Caulfield, an energetic and inquisitive man by nature, was born Malachy Francis Caulfield in Belfast in 1923. As a Catholic growing up in a strongly Protestant and Pro-British community, he shortened his name to Max while he was still at school and adopted this permanently when he became a journalist on the *Belfast Telegraph*. After service in the British Army during the Second World War, he settled in England and became a familiar figure in London's Fleet Street during the 1950s, 1960s and 1970s, writing for several of the national newspapers.

In 1952, Caulfield published his first novel, *The Black City*, drawing on his own background and featuring an IRA man whose girl friend wants him to quit the terrorist organisation, but is unable to do so before he dies in action. Although attacked and praised by reviewers in equal measure – one said it was 'marred by coarseness and irreverence', another hailed it for 'not sparing the IRA' – the novel contains a memorable introductory paragraph that has frequently been quoted:

It was the Black City because of what is between Protestant and Catholic, between British mongrel and mongrel Irishman, that is narrow hated and bigotry. It is not much of a place as cities go, a nineteenth-century industrial profusion of shipyards and gantries, linen-mills, factory chimneys, flaking pubs, oily river basins and mile after mile of narrow, mean streets.

A decade later, Caulfield proved himself to be an equally skilled and adept writer of non-fiction when he published a scrupulously researched narrative history, *The Easter Rebellion: Dublin 1916* (1963), which was critically acclaimed and reprinted several times. Among other titles which underlined Caulfield's versatility, as well as his ability to uncover facts, must be included *A Night of Terror: The Story of the Athenia Affair* (1962), *The Irish Mystique* (1973) and the extraordinary biography of *The Beast of Jersey* (1972), a mass-murderer who kept a secret room for black magic rituals and attacked his victims wearing a hideous rubber mask and nail-studded bracelets. The book was 'ghosted' by Caulfield with the man's wife, Joan Paisnel, and it has proved the precursor of a whole range of books about serial killers. Apart from the books, Max Caulfield also wrote feature-length articles for the Fleet Street newspapers, in particular the *Sunday Dispatch*.

It was in the first week of November 1960 that the paper advertised a 'sensational new series' – THE SPEAR OF DESTINY – HOW HITLER LIVED BY THE WEAPON THRUST INTO CHRIST. Underneath Max Caulfield's by-line was the claim, 'Revealed for the first time the incredible truth about Hitler's worship of the Devil. This talisman, he thought, would bring to his aid all the Powers of Darkness.'

For the readers of the *Dispatch* who opened their paper on the morning of Sunday, 6 November, what followed must have seemed more like fiction than fact – although Caulfield was quick to cite his major source early in the article:

This amazing, untold story of the war was revealed to me last week. The widow of a noted Austrian historian and lecturer, Dr Walter Johannes Stein, opened her husband's unpublished archives to me. They show that Hitler was obsessed by a desire to possess the spear. In his mad, twisted brain, the German Führer believed that he could harness its mystic power and it became his secret talisman.

The author stated that by carefully studying the notes left by Dr Stein and his associates it been possible for him to present a true picture of Hitler's 'devil worship' and explain how the spear of Longinus came to be at the centre of his beliefs. Why had these facts about his life never been revealed before? Historians had certainly probed every secret of the Nazis, Caulfield said, but this was the one carefully guarded secret that had 'never been more than hinted at until today'.

According to the doctor's notes, Hitler had become influenced by the occult and the Black Arts while a drifter in Vienna and further still as a shell-shocked victim from the First World War. As the Nazi Party grew, he began to rely increasingly on the German occult brotherhood to help keep control of his top aides.

At the forefront of this group, Stein claimed, was a Viennese occultist named Guido von Liszt, the leader of a 'Blood Lodge' who practised black magic and sexual perversions. Born in 1848, the son of a dealer in leather goods, he had developed an obsession with the idea of the Germans as a heroic race of blue-eyed, blond warriors. He also believed himself to be the last survivor of a secret society of magicians, the Armanen, whose purpose was to restore the greatness of the Nordic type. While still in his teens, Liszt had apparently crept before the altar in the crypt in St Stephen's Cathedral in Vienna, renounced his Catholic faith and sworn to build a temple to the ancient god, Wotan.

For some years, as Liszt became an increasingly

eccentric-looking figure with a long, flowing white beard that reached right down to his waist, he scraped a meagre living as a journalist and author of a number of books about Pan-Germanic mysticism. Notable among these were *German Mythological Landscapes* (1891) and the *Secret of the Runes* (1908), which attracted a modest readership and earned him the reputation of the 'father of *volkisch* occultism'.

Then, in 1909, Liszt was exposed in the press as the mastermind of an underground occult group that employed the swastika instead of the cross in magic rituals and had used the body of a naked prostitute to try to raise a demon in a ceremony designed to create a 'Moon Child'. He had, it seemed, also been using the swastika as a symbol of racial purity and neo-paganism for over a quarter of a century a fact not lost on his later followers in the embryo Nazi Party. When news of these activities was spread across the front page of the *Arbeiter-Zeitung*, von Liszt fled to Germany.

Once safely across the border, the ageing mystic began secretly rebuilding his Lodge – contacting some of his former associates still bound by their 'blood oath' that prevented them from leaving the group on pain of death. He also started seeking new recruits, a process that was helped by the demoralising effects of the First World War and a desire among certain sections of the population for magical experiences. By the time Hitler came to power, Dr Stein told Max Caulfield, the group was powerful once again:

This Nazi 'blood lodge' met to perform secret rites in veneration of Hitler. A token of his blood was used in the ceremonies. Among the members were Julius Streicher, the prime Jew-baiter; Alfred Rosenberg, the race theorist; Heinrich Himmler, chief of the Gestapo; and Hermann Goering, swaggering chief of the Luftwaffe. With Hitler, these men sought a diabolical power by perverting everything holy: their swastika was a deliberately inverted image of an early Christian symbol: their lust for the Holy Spear was governed by the same principles. They wanted to harness its power.

The spear was, of course, still far from Hitler's grasp – in Vienna. But once he had decided to invade Austria in 1938, he knew he would soon be able to do more than just gaze at the relic in a glass case. According to Dr Stein, the Führer believed that as soon as the relic was in his possession he would be 'able to use the magic talisman to make himself master of the world'.

Hitler's rumoured magical powers had caught the attention of other historians, Caulfield said, though he did not mention his sources. He might well have taken the words of Alan Bullock who had written in 1952: 'Hitler's power to bewitch an audience has been likened to the occult arts of the African medicine-man or the Asiatic shaman.' Since then, Francis King has been even more specific about him in *Satan and Swastika: The Occult in the Nazi Party* (1976):

There is another aspect of the Führer's activities which has fascinated some contemporary occultists. He was, they say, a master of ritual magic, the art and science of producing changes of consciousness in accordance with will. They are not saying, save in one or two cases, that he practised the sort of magic associated with either primitive witchcraft or the medieval *grimoires*, or arguing that he clad himself in white robes, drew a magic circle and chanted 'barbarous words of evocation' until such time as a demon chose to physically manifest itself. What they do suggest is that Hitler had either learned from others the same techniques of consciousness-alteration as was employed by the ritual magicians of such modern fraternities as the Golden Dawn and the Kabalistic Rose-Croix.

At this point in Max Caulfield's report he introduced another of the important players in the drama – SS Colonel Conrad Buch, Head of the *Oberstes Parteigericht*, a man who had been a lawyer in peacetime and was now a personal adviser to Hitler. A thin, sinister Prussian, he had gained the Führer's confidence by ruthlessly destroying Freemasonry in Germany and compiling a dossier on the power of the Roman Catholic Church throughout the country. He was also a man with more than passing interest in the object of the mission that he was entrusted with, as Caulfield wrote:

Dr Stein found that Buch was one of the elite Nazis who shared Hitler's fabulous belief in the world beyond normal understanding: the secret, dangerous world of the occult. He knew all about the spear that his leader craved to own and shared his belief in its power.

Even before Hitler put his plan for seizing Austria into effect, he despatched Buch to Vienna on a covert mission. He was to ensure that the spear and the other precious relics of the ancient German Empire, the *Reichskleinodien*, were not spirited away before he arrived as they had been in the past when other invaders had loomed on the horizon. Hitler told the SS colonel he wanted to receive the spear *personally* on the day he next entered the Schatzkammer.

Buch arrived in Vienna several days ahead of the *Anschluss* on 12 March disguised as a businessman. He drove to a small hotel, a quarter of a mile from the museum, and booked a room. Inside his innocent-looking suitcase was his SS uniform, a Luger pistol he had become proficient at using, and his secret orders. He was specifically instructed to kill anyone who might attempt to frustrate the Führer's ambition.

For more than a week, Buch mingled among the crowds of sightseers who visited the museum all the time unaware of what the future had in store for them. He studied the layout of the rooms with typical Prussian thoroughness and occasionally slipped back unobtrusively into Room 11 where the spear and the other items of regalia lay. He was leaving nothing to chance.

Then on the night of the *Anschluss* as Field Marshal Wilhelm Keitel's 8th Army Group and several of the famous Panzer Divisions crossed the border into Austria, Buch moved quickly into action. A party of Nazi storm troopers in the first wave of German soldiers to reach Vienna had been assigned to him – and he knew they had explicit instructions to follow his orders to the letter. Once the men had arrived, he changed into his full military uniform and marched down the Ringstrasse into the Kunsthistorisches Museum. No one challenged the black-suited party of men as they strode into the Schatzkammer.

Within an hour the Colonel and the storm troopers had gathered up into cases all the items of the *Reichskleinodien* – taking especial care with the fragile spear that Buch kept separate. He wanted everything to be just right when the Führer arrived in Vienna.

The Führer's arrival, though, was not expected until the following day. First, he wanted to visit his birthplace, Linz, and place a wreath on the grave of his mother at Leonding. Hitler, increasingly cautious where his own safety and dignity was concerned, also wanted to allow time for additional security measures to be put in place in the city to weed out any possible anti-Nazi demonstrators or assassins.

Caulfield then described another significant moment in the long history of the holy lance:

Huge crowds of over 200,000 people cheered the entry of Hitler into Vienna. He drove to the reviewing stand in front of the Hofburg where he reviewed the Austrian SS and accepted the adulation of the people. That evening, at a glittering reception held in the Royal Place, Colonel Buch delivered the spear to his Führer. The guests were toasting the Nazi success in champagne as Buch and his party entered. They bore the spear across the crowded reception room to face Adolf Hitler.

Clicking his heels, Colonel Buch threw up a thin arm in the Nazi salute and spoke, '*Die Heilige Lance, mein Führer.*' The effect was electric. A silence almost of awe fell upon the gathering as he solemnly presented his trophy. As had been done to all the Habsburg emperors, Hitler allowed himself to be touched with it upon the shoulder.

According to Dr Stein, a number of the Austrian nobles in the room stirred uneasily. They looked anxiously from one another as their new ruler held the spear in his hands, his eyes glittering with pleasure as if he had at last found something he had desired for years – which, of course, he had. But to some of the men in the room that night the act they had just witnessed seemed almost *blasphemous*. For was this not a man obsessed with using the occult and the supernatural in his quest for power? The words he then spoke to the assembled company did little to quell these anxieties:

I feel the call of Providence has come to me. I have been charged with a mission to reunite the German People – to join my homeland to the Reich. I have believed in this Mission. I have lived for it and I believe I have now fulfilled it. Tomorrow may every German recognise the hour and measure its importance and bow in humility before the Almighty, who in a few weeks has wrought such as miracle upon us.

At that moment – Dr Walter Johannes Stein was to write in his notes many years later – he began to fear that Hitler planned to use the spear not for good as so many of those before him had done, but for evil. Armed with this symbol of invincibility, nothing would be beyond his powers. As a result of his own study of Dr Stein's notes, Caulfield believed he was also able to explain the hidden significance of the Führer's curious statement:

Only those who shared Hitler's black secrets guessed their true meaning. He was not giving thanks to God. He was raising his prayer of gratitude to the Forces of Darkness. In this supreme blasphemy, he linked his faith and his future with them. With the spear of destiny by his side, he gave thanks to the Devil.

One report of the time suggested that Hitler spent an hour alone with the spear – just as he had done a quarter of a century earlier. He sent everyone out of the room – his entourage as well as all the Austrian officials and invited guests – while he silently contemplated the little spearhead in his hands.

True or not, Max Caulfield said that Dr Stein's evidence indicated that Hitler kept the spear jealously beside him for 'many months' once it was in his possession. As one European nation after another fell before the *blitzkrieg* of his army and air force, the Führer had every reason to believe in its powers of invincibility. Even during the time when the embattled island of England and her few remaining allies held fast, it seemed nothing could now halt his plans for world domination.

Indeed, for the next few years the power of Hitler and the spear seemed absolute. But, as Caulfield was to reveal in the second part of his investigation, *Die Heilige Lanz* was also to influence Hitler in ways he could never have imagined.

What the writer did *not* reveal was Dr Stein's involvement with Winston Churchill and the statesman's interest in the spear. In particular, the actions the British prime minister took to ensure that the Nazi leader did not use it to realise his terrifying ambition.

Seven

The Churchill Connection

Kensington, in the heart of London, with its famous Gardens and rows of stylish town houses in little enclaves behind both sides of the bustling High Street, has been home to many distinguished foreign exiles. From the late nineteenth century through to the Second World War, numerous men, woman and children driven from their homes in Europe and elsewhere have come here to escape persecution and build new lives for themselves in a country that is one of the few constant centres of freedom to be found in the world.

Dr Paul Tabori, an exiled Hungarian was such man. Born in Budapest in 1908, he had gained a doctorate in economic and political science at the city's university in 1930 and worked as a journalist and literary agent. Then, with the threat of the Nazis looming, he moved to London in 1938 and made his home in Kensington at Stafford Terrace. A short, bespectacled man with a moustache and an easy smile, Paul became a familiar figure on the London literary scene during and after the war as a writer of often-controversial books about prophecy and the occult. He was also a friend of Dr Johannes Walter Stein, the man who knew all about Hitler and the Spear of Longinus and was the prime source of information later drawn on by Max Caulfield and Trevor Ravenscroft.

Tabori's interest in and attitude towards Germany was evident in his first novel, *They Came To London* (1943), a near-future story of the Second Front, and his inside information about the nation and its leader was further revealed in *The Private Life of Adolf Hitler* which he published in 1949. In subsequent years his knowledge of the supernatural and the occult, which he had been developing since his youth, lead to him becoming the editor of a series of radical books on the latest research into ghosts, spiritualism and magic. The fact that he was vice-president of the Ghost Club and the Literary Executor of the Estate of Harry Price – one of the great psychic investigators of the last century who had bequeathed his unrivalled library of books, documents and photographs to University College, London – made Tabori a magnet for people investigating such subjects. I count myself privileged to have been among this group of people during the later years of his life.

It was, therefore, perhaps inevitable that Dr Stein and he should meet. Not just because they lived near one another – Dr Stein's house was just the other side of Kensington High Street in Pembroke Gardens – but because both shared an interest in Hitler's obsession with the occult. It is thanks to Paul Tabori's enquiries that we have details of Dr Stein and his wartime work for the prime minister Winston Churchill.

Walter Johannes Stein was born in Vienna in 1891. His father was a barrister who specialised in International Law and briefly hoped his son would follow in his footsteps. Instead young Walter went to the Technische Universitat on the Getreide Markt where he studied mathematics and physics and also became interested in the occult.

The First World War interrupted Stein's studies, but he still managed to write his PhD dissertation on philosophy in 1918 while serving in the Imperial Austrian Army on the Russian front. Against this chaotic background where he attained the rank of captain and was decorated for bravery, he produced a groundbreaking doctorial thesis that related the higher levels of consciousness to the human organs and the biochemistry of the body – anticipating psycho-physical research that would occur almost half a century later.

Throughout this period of his life, Stein's fascination with the occult grew. His interest particularly focused on the legend of the Holy Grail and it, in turn, led him to the Spear of Longinus. Several times he made the short journey from the university to the museum in the Hofburg, to study the agate bowl with its pattern of the name of Christ displayed in Room 8, and the *Heilige*

Lanze three rooms away. There is a report that he was actually in the same room when Hitler saw the spear for the very first time – but there is no evidence to substantiate this claim.

After the war, Dr Stein began teaching history and literature at the first Waldorf School opened in Stuttgart in 1919 under the direction of Rudolf Steiner. It was in Germany, too, that he began to build his reputation as an expert on medieval history – as well as beginning work on a book about the Holy Grail. In this he sought to establish a connection between actual historic events and those episodes portrayed in the European 'Grail Sagas' of the twelfth and thirteenth centuries – in particular von Eschenbach's *Parsifal*. The outcome was *Das Neunte Jahrhunderf und Weltgeschichte im Lichte des Heiligen Gral* (*The Ninth Century and the Holy Grail*) a 'book of the Grail for the Twentieth Century' to quote the publisher's blurb – which was issued in Stuttgart at Easter, 1928, and has since been described as one of the definitive works on the subject.

In the book Dr Stein cited several references to the holy lance in Parsifal and left the reader in no doubt as to the extensive research he had carried out while writing the text. He noted in an afterword:

The lance here portrayed as an imaginative picture within Parsifal's vision is also an historical and physical object. The Centurion Longinus, who pierced the side of Christ on the Cross and gave rise to a legend which comes from Zobingen near Ellwangen, first used it. The Syrian Ephraim in the 39th Hymn of his so-called Nisibinian Hymns brings this lance into connection with the lance of Phineas. He says the lance originally guarded the Tree of Life. Adam, who had fallen, returned to Paradise through it.

The author then summarised the history of the spear as I have given it in these pages and listed the rulers and kings who had owned it. He also made mention of three other lances – apart from the one in Vienna – in Rome, Cracow and Armenia to which we shall be returning later. Stein's reference to the legend having begun in Germany is also interesting in that it may well have been the source of the suggestion that Longinus was of Germanic descent.

Dr Stein continued his teaching and research in Germany during the 1930s, and was also in demand as a lecturer, economist and as the editor of a current affairs magazine published in English, *The Present Age*, which he ran from 1935 until the outbreak of the war. In the interim, he also made several trips to London – notably in 1936 when he was asked to accompany King Leopold of the Belgians to deliver one of the earliest speeches advocating a Common Market. All the time, though, he was growing more apprehensive about what was happening in Germany under the new Nazi regime.

Later, when Stein had settled in London, he revealed more of his earlier life to fellow exile Dr Paul Tabori during the years of their friendship that lasted until his death in 1957. Tabori, in fact, became the second writer to present details of Hitler's obsession with the spear – and the first to reveal the role of Winston Churchill. This was contained in an article for the London *Evening News* in December 1972. It was written to break the news about the book to which his late friend had contributed, *The Spear of Destiny* by Trevor Ravenscroft, then due to be published the following spring. The article made sensational Christmas reading, with Tabori claiming that his friend had told him of meeting Hitler in a second-hand bookshop in Vienna:

Stein belonged to a mystical society which developed clairvoyance in its members and from his first encounter, the Doctor judged that the down-at-heel Hitler had a quite extraordinary potential for evil. He met Hitler at intervals for more than a year and they discussed magic, Black and White, together. He saw Hitler go into a trance and contact what he believed to be evil spirits of great powers'.

Later, wrote Tabori, the group were able to observe, clairvoyantly, the rituals through which the Nazi movement was being brought to power. However, the 'inner cabinet' of the Nazi Party believed that three of its members – Dietrich Eckhart, Professor Karl

Haushofer, and Hitler himself – had 'developed superhuman powers'. The men also knew that their most secret meetings were being monitored in the same way. The article continued:

Himmler gave orders to liquidate this danger, but Stein knew in advance and escaped to Belgium. Many of his colleagues were rounded up and killed. The destruction of this group of mystics was, in fact, the first Nazi *pogrom* and took priority in the Nazi timetable over Jews and Gypsies.

Doctor Stein made his way to London where a reader of *The Present Age* helped him to find a home in Pembroke Gardens. Here he assembled a huge collection of books on history and occultism that eventually spilled from one room into the next. In his lounge above the fireplace hung a print of Rembrandt's 'Red Knight of the Grail' depicting the great warrior carrying the holy spear. It was one of his favourite possessions.

Stein's friends also helped him to find an office in nearby Beaufort Gardens to practise psychology. However, said Tabori, within months of his arrival in London this was being used as a 'front', as British Intelligence had recruited the doctor. His knowledge of the Nazi Party was invaluable and with the connivance of the authorities he made at least one secret trip back to Europe. His neighbour and friend wrote:

Suggestions that the Nazi movement had its roots in a major Black Magic operation – and hints that some individuals in Britain were aware of this – have been current in Europe, particularly in France, since the middle Fifties. It has generally been claimed that no documentation to support such an incredible idea could possibly be produced. Doctor Stein, though, had been sent back to Europe once the war started and the information he produced on his return triggered off alarm signals to the West.

There is convincing proof, too, that the polite and self-effacing doctor with his gold-rimmed glasses who looked more like a respectable professor than an enemy agent, secured some other invaluable information on this trip. Nothing less than the outline details of *Operation Seelowe* (Operation Sea lion) the secret German invasion plans for England. These were immediately passed to Winston Churchill and his advisers for the closest scrutiny.

From the moment of his return, Dr Walter Stein became the prime minister's 'most secret and least suspected adviser on the mind and motives of Hitler and the leading members of the Nazi Party', according to Tabori. He reported regularly to a small group of advisers who evaluated all the information that came their way about the Führer and his obsession with the occult – 'material which in ordinary political circles would have been dismissed out of hand'.

The names of these men who met Stein during the war years have never been revealed – though among their number are believed to have been John Buchan who wrote two attacks on the German interest in magical forces, 'The Judgement of Dawn' and 'A Prince in Captivity'; Hilary St George Saunders whose books *Seven Sleepers* and *The Hidden Kingdom* denounced the dark menace of Nazi esotericism, and Rudyard Kipling who demanded that the swastika symbol which had appeared on the covers of his novels for years should now be removed.

Tabori wrote that it was Winston Churchill who personally gave orders that the activities of all Germans believed to be associated with occultism in the Third Reich should be monitored. Anything peculiar or bizarre that was discovered should by used in whatever way best suited the British cause. The options were twofold: to ridicule such ideas or turn the supernaturalism back against its perpetrators. What should not be done was to dismiss the whole subject out of hand.

The fact remains that despite the prime minister's huge workload and his immensely realistic and practical nature, he retained an open mind on the occult. He was a man who believed in destiny – his own as well as other people's – and was well briefed on Hitler's bizarre obsessions. He knew, for example, that the Führer had his own astrologer whom he frequently consulted, as Francis King has written in his book, *Satan and Swastika*:

So seriously were such reports taken in London that during the autumn of 1940 and the spring of 1941, the British War Office went to the length of employing a professional astrologer, a certain Louis de Wohl, in the hope that by the study of Hitler's horoscope he could anticipate Hitler's next move. Such a hope was not quite so silly as it might seem to have been: for it is a fact that many of Hitler's major initiatives were undertaken at times when by chance it happened that his progressed horoscope gave favourable indications for success.

The air of mystery surrounding the group of which Dr Stein was a part was in fact deliberate. It was all part of a 'cover-up' of the information about Hitler's occultism. Indeed, even when the war was over, Winston Churchill insisted that the facts should remain secret, as Paul Tabori's article explained:

Churchill believed that the real nature of the conflict between Germany and the West was so incredible that any attempt to disclose the facts would simply be ridiculed. At the end of the war a 'hush-up' policy was agreed at the highest level and the Nuremberg Trials were arranged so as to present the top Nazis as 'ordinary criminals'. The big secret was one, Churchill said, 'that must never in any circumstances become public knowledge.'

And what was the secret Churchill thought the world must not be told? It was that Hitler's circle believed that in return for a deluge of blood and destruction they would contact energies capable of triggering off a mutation in the human species. This would then breed a new – and Satanic – species of man. The specially bred, blond elite of the SS were being trained in the Brandenburg Organisation in Berlin to receive this genetic change. The Master Race would following – not as a figure of speech, but as a biological fact. The rest of the human race would become a slave race.

Even after the Nuremberg Trials in 1946, Stein tried to get the Prime Minister to change his mind, but Churchill remained adamant. The materialistic nature of the West would make it impossible for the revelations to be taken seriously, he said, and the Western world would lose the lesson which, later, it might be able to learn. From then until the Viennese doctor's death, pressure was kept on him to commit nothing whatsoever to paper about his wartime experiences.

But, said Paul Tabori in closing his article, another writer, Trevor Ravenscroft, had also been given access to the 'suitcase full of papers' that Dr Stein's widow, Eliza, had first shown to Max Caulfield. There Ravenscroft had apparently discovered even more evidence about Hitler and the influence of the occult in the Third Reich. After years of research of his own, he was now about to publish a book disclosing the true extent of the Führer's interest – and, in particular, his obsession with the holy lance of Longinus. *The Spear of Destiny* would also reveal the facts about the roles played by some of Hitler's closest and most sinister associates in this period of its history.

In recent years, anyone who has become interested in the legend of the holy spear will more than likely have consulted Trevor Ravenscroft's book, *The Spear of Destiny*. In it he describes the occult power that lay behind the spear and how Hitler inverted this force in his bid to conquer the world. On publication in 1973, the book became a bestseller in Britain and America and was translated into over a dozen foreign languages.

Ravenscoft, a tall, heavily bearded man with almost messianic eyes was, in many ways, as fascinating and enigmatic as the book he wrote. Born to a well-to-do English family in 1921, he was educated at Repton and then gained entrance to Sandhurst Military Academy where he was regarded as an exemplary student. When the Second World War broke out, he joined the newly formed Commandos and was sent with a detachment commanded by Lieutenant Colonel Geoffrey Keyes to North Africa where the British Forces were then fighting a desperate rearguard action against Field Marshal Erwin Rommel's all-conquering Panzer troops.

According to Ravenscroft, when the Germans were threatening to over-run Libya and storm into Egypt in order to seize the Suez Canal, Lt Colonel Keyes was asked to lead an assassination attempt on Rommel's life. He was a member of this ill-fated group and was one of the commandos captured by the Germans. His fate was to be transported to Germany where he was a prisoner-of-war from 1941 to 1945. By his own account, he escaped three times but was recaptured each time. Ravenscroft's imprisonment was, though, to have a profound effect on his life in a most unexpected way, as he later explained:

> While I was in this Nazi camp I read a great deal about the occult and also developed my higher levels of consciousness. The nature of this transcendent experience guided me to a study of the Holy Grail and to research the history of the Spear of Longinus and the legend of world destiny which had grown around it.

At the end of the war, Ravenscroft returned to London a changed man. For a time he studied at St Thomas' Hospital while continuing to follow up clues about the Holy Grail and the spear. Among the most influential books he came across was Dr Stein's *The Ninth Century and the Holy Grail* and this inspired his first protracted enquiry into the possible whereabouts of the fabled cup that had collected the blood of Christ. His search took him to Rosslyn in Midlothian where a group of Templars who had fled to Scotland had built a cemetery. Historian Chris Thornborrow in his article,

'An Introduction to Current Theories about the Holy Grail', has described what transpired:

> The famous Grail seeker Trevor Ravenscroft claimed in 1962 that he had finished a 20-year quest in search of the Grail at Rosslyn Chapel. His claim was that the Grail was inside the Prentice Pillar (as it is known) in this chapel. The chapel is often visited now by Grail Seekers and many references to the Grail can be found in its stonework and windows. Metal detectors have been used on the pillar and an object of the appropriate size *is* buried in the middle. However, Lord Rosslyn adamantly refuses to have the pillar x-rayed.

Convinced that he had found the solution to the mystery, Ravenscroft then turned his attention to the other half of his obsession – the Spear of Longinus. According to his version of events in *The Spear of Destiny*, he tracked down Dr Stein to his London address and was 'in close contact with him until he died in 1957'. The author's biography on the dust jacket of his book also claims that he 'studied history under Dr Walter Johannes Stein for twelve years' and had been carrying out extensive research into the subject ever since 1945. However, investigative writer Eric Wynants claimed in an article written in 1982 that 'the conversations I had with Ravenscroft included [his] admission that he never met W.J. Stein, but "talked to him only via a medium".'

Unfortunately, Ravenscroft died in 1989, so there is no way of clarifying which of these statements is correct. Retired London publisher Neville Armstrong who issued *The Spear of Destiny* under his appropriately named Neville Spearman imprint, has very mixed feelings about the author with whom he spent several years working to bring the book to completion. 'He was', says Armstrong in his privately published autobiography, *Catching Up With The Future* (1999) 'certainly the most difficult and devious malchick I have ever published'.

After giving Ravenscroft a £2,000 advance to write the book – no mean figure in 1971 says Armstrong – the author 'disappeared without trace'. Eventually tracked down to a fisherman's cottage in Cornwall, the writer claimed to be penniless with no money for food for himself and his wife and he could not even send his child to school because 'there was nothing to buy proper shoes or clothing.' Ravenscroft made no mention whatsoever of the money he had already been given to write the book. Armstrong continues:

> We then offered him further weekly payments until the manuscript was completed. He was really rather a foolish, twisted chap who had considerable esoteric knowledge, wrongly used. The story of the spear eventually became a best-seller, the American rights of which I sold to William Targ of Putnam's for $50,000.

Neville Armstrong also remembers being introduced to pot by Ravenscroft, a habitual user. Indeed, the publisher's experience might well explain the origin of some of the more outlandish flights of fantasy to be found in *The Spear of Destiny*!

Trevor Ravenscroft was, though, gracious enough to admit in his Foreword to the *The Spear of Destiny* that the book should really have been written by Dr Stein, whose widow had given him access to all the Austrian's painstakingly assembled information and papers. It was important that this evidence was made public, Ravenscroft said, because considerable pressure had been brought to bear on Dr Stein to keep silent about the contents of the book:

But in the final issue he was not influenced in any way by such external persuasion. Not even by the instance of Churchill himself who was insistent that the occultism of the Nazi Party should not under any circumstances be revealed to the general public.

Unquestionably, Trevor Ravenscroft used Stein's material to go into much more detail than Max Caulfield had the time – or inclination – to do, in particular on the question of the other occultists who had been responsible for Hitler's fixation with the spear. He agreed that Guido von Liszt had been an early influence, but pointed the finger much more directly at two other men, Dietrich Eckardt and Professor Karl

Haushofer. Here again, he was not quite the first, as an earlier, highly regarded work on the occult written in 1960, *The Dawn of Magic* by the French writers, Louis Pauwels and Jacques Bergier, had also named the pair.

Eckardt, a glowering, bald man with a heavy black moustache, has been called the 'spiritual founder of Nazism'. Certainly he was Hitler's mentor: Hitler referred to him in *Mein Kampf* as 'one of the best who devoted his life to the awakening of our people, in his writings, his thoughts and finally in his deeds'. It was that mention of 'awakening' and those 'thoughts and deeds' that Dr Stein considered made him such a sinister presence.

Born in 1868, Dietrich Eckardt struggled to make a living as a poet, playwright and journalist in the years prior to the First World War. Then, like Hitler, he was badly injured by mustard gas while serving in the trenches and forced to take morphine to overcome the pain along with liberal amounts of alcohol. In 1919 he revealed himself to be a strident anti-Semite in a pamphlet, *Auf Gut Deutsch* (*In Plain German*), printing 25,000 copies at his own expense and distributing them to all those of a 1ike mind. These, though, were not the only similarities he had with the man he would so profoundly influence, as Konrad Heiden has written in *Der Führer* (1945):

> Eckardt was the same sort of uprooted, agitated and far from immaculate soul. In Berlin, already in his

Thirties, he had led the life of a vagrant who believes himself to be a poet. He could tell Hitler that he (like Hitler himself) had lodged in countless flophouses and slept on park benches because of Jewish machinations which, in his case, had prevented him from becoming a successful playwright.

The two men first met in 1920 at Richard Wagner's house in Beyruth and during the next three years – says Heiden – 'Eckardt undertook the spiritual formation of Adolph Hitler. His instruction was given on two levels: one being concerned with the "Secret Doctrine" and the other with the doctrine of propaganda.'

This secret doctrine was the art of the occult, at which Eckardt was already a practised adept and a leading figure in the Thule Group dedicated to using magic to propel the Aryan race to glory. He, too, had studied the legend of the Holy Grail and the Spear of Longinus and believed they could be vital in achieving world domination for the German people. When he and Hitler came to discuss the spear and their obsession with the relic, Eckardt at once urged him to do everything he could to bring it back from Vienna to its rightful home in Nuremberg.

In 1923, Eckardt became one of the founding members of the National Socialist Party. Within months, however, the toll of morphine addiction and alcohol abuse resulted in his death – but not before he had time to pass on a message to his followers and friends that revealed both his ego and his prophetic vision about what lay ahead:

> Follow Hitler! He will dance, but it is I who have called the tune. I have initiated him into the Secret Doctrine, opened his centres of vision and given him the means to communicate with the Powers. Do not mourn me, for I shall have influenced history more than any other German.

One of Eckardt's closest friends, Professor Karl Haushofer, was at his bedside to hear these ominous words. A small, deceptively benign-looking man, but possessing unnerving, hooded eyes, he was also capable of extraordinary prophecies. Haushofer was the second man to further Hitler's interest in the spear and also, legend has it, the person who proposed the swastika as the emblem for the embryo Nazi Party. Ravenscroft writes of him:

> Haushofer, the Master Magician of the Nazi Party, was instrumental in initiating the Führer into a perception of how the evil powers worked within the historical process. It was he, too, who encouraged Hitler to remove the Spear of Destiny from the Hofburg in Vienna and to place it in Nuremberg, from whence its powers could emanate from the very heart of the Nazi movement.

The little professor was born in Bavaria in 1869 and initially chose to be a professional soldier where his striking intellect and quick grasp of languages earned him rapid promotion. For several years he worked for the German Intelligence Service in India, the Far East and Japan, where he became increasingly fascinated by mysticism. While in Japan, he is said to have been initiated into a secret society and sworn that if he failed in his 'mystical mission' to promote the 'Secret Doctrine', he would commit suicide.

In the East, too, he became convinced that the Germanic race had originated in Central Asia and in order to preserve the superiority of the German *Herrenvolk*, the Reich would have to expand eastwards. He would later illustrate this theory in his writings with a map of a swastika expanding across Europe and beyond.

On his return to Germany, Haushofer studied at the University of Munich for a doctorate – which he obtained with a ground-breaking thesis on Political Geography – but was then called up on the outbreak of the First World War to serve on the Western Front. He proved an outstanding general, as well as possessing a remarkable gift for being able to predict events before they happened: events such as political changes in countries about which he knew nothing, the hour in which the enemy would attack, and even the spots on which their shells would fall.

Following Germany's defeat, Haushofer returned to

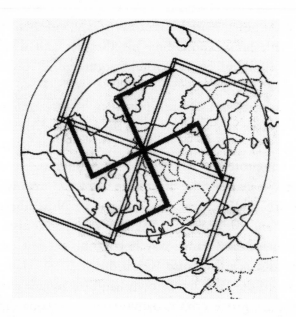

7 *The Expanding World of the Swastika* by Professor Karl Haushofer

the University of Munich as Professor of Geopolitics
to expound his beliefs and in 1921 founded the *Geo-
Political Review* that espoused a new dawn for the
nation. Here he gained a new assistant named
Rudolph Hess who would later claim that the
professor was not only a mystic of great power but
also a secret chief. Hess introduced him to his close
friend, Adolf Hitler, who would later make his
number two in the Reich. Pauwels and Bergier
write:

After his abortive rising, Hitler was confined to
prison at Landshurt. Introduced by Hess,

Haushofer visited Hitler every day and spent hours with him expounding his theories and deducing from them every possible argument in favour of political conquest. Left alone with Hess, Hitler amalgamated, for the purposes of propaganda, the theories of Haushofer and the basis of *Mein Kampf*.

The professor would live long enough to see Hitler achieve many of the dreams he had for Germany – the return of the Spear of Longinus to Nuremberg, for one, and the fulfilling of German expansionism in a manner and distance way beyond his wildest dreams. He also saw the Third Reich die. In 1946, Haushofer himself died and by his own hand – a suicide credited in some quarters to the oath that he had sworn all those years before as a secret initiate in Japan.

The news that Hitler had taken possession of the Spear of Longinus after he had annexed Austria in March 1938 was reported to Winston Churchill in a secret memo written by Dr Walter Stein. The document stuck very much to the facts of the seizure of the *Reichkleinodien* and its return to Germany under guard by handpicked SS troops. Hitler had, though, the doctor said, made a token attempt to justify this action by citing the decree of Emperor Sigismund that the relics should 'never leave the soil of the Fatherland'.

Stein reported that all the items of royal regalia including the spear had been transported from Vienna to Germany on an armoured train and were to go on display in the Nazi heartland at Nuremberg. The ancient St Katherine's Church had been selected as a suitable venue and already there were reports that people were gathering in their thousands to view the latest jewels in the Führer's crown. Trevor Ravenscroft has written the finale on this particular chapter in the story of the spear:

> Only the solitary voice of Winston Churchill warned the world that Hitler's entry into Vienna constituted such a decisive change in the balance of European power that world war was now inevitable. In possession, through Dr Walter Stein, of all the facts regarding Adolf Hitler's fascination with the legend of world destiny associated with the Reich's Lance in the Hofburg, Winston Churchill could see with an even greater transparency the Nazi's Führer's plans for world conquest.

As he read the details of his enemy's delight at finally owning the relic, it is not difficult to imagine that the British Prime Minister must have known in his heart that peace would not return to Europe until the spear was out of Hitler's hands once again...

Eight

Fatal Date with Destiny

The ominous drone of dozens of RAF bombers was audible for some minutes before the menacing shapes of the aircraft themselves became visible in the moonlit sky over the ancient walled city of Nuremberg. It was an unfamiliar sight and sound to the people living there and many were roused from their beds to peer up into the darkened heavens. Surprise was soon mixed with anxiety – for despite what the radio had repeatedly told them that the cities of Germany were impregnable, there was still gossip that the supposedly embattled British were now sending over ever-increasing numbers of aircraft to bomb the Fatherland. Each day these planes were said to be penetrating further and further into the heartland of the Reich.

On the night of 28–9 August 1942 these rumours became reality when high-explosive bombs and incendiaries fell for the first time on 'the Spiritual Home of Nazism' as Hitler and his cohorts liked to think of Nuremberg. This raid – the first of a total that would rise to thirty-eight – was to prove a particular blow to the prestige of the Führer, as well as a threat to the Spear of Longinus which had been moved there four years earlier from Vienna and was now regarded as a symbol of Hitler's triumph and the confirmation of his stature as a man of destiny.

The city of Nuremberg had, in fact, been inextricably linked with the Nazi Party for almost a decade. To members of the movement it was also connected with some of the most significant developments in German history: in particular, the former German empire, expressions of patriotic sentiment and now the massed gatherings that had earned it the epithet of 'City of Rallies' to match Munich's 'Capital of the Party' and Berlin's 'Capital of the Reich'.

It was in September 1933, that the first Nazi Party Congress had been held in Nuremberg In the years that followed, a mixture of verbal propaganda, martial music, parades and thousands of swastika flags were guaranteed to overwhelm the senses of everyone who visited the city. Up to a million party members would crowd inside the old walls to visit the geomantically designed, Roman-style stadium, the Tannenberg, which had been specially created on the Führer's instructions to resemble the Altar of Zeus at Pergamum in west Turkey. Through this vast auditorium would parade endless ranks of goose-stepping Brownshirts, SS storm troopers, Labour Corps, Hitler Youth and army, navy and air force personnel, all intended to demonstrate the might of the Thousand-Year Reich.

The march-pasts could take anything up to eight hours and served a dual purpose: they intimidated any opposition within Germany or countries abroad and, some argue, raised vast psychic energies that were manipulated by Hitler with his occult knowledge to ensure his iron grip on the nation. Never before had such vast acts of ritual magic been seen anywhere on this awesome scale.

The Rallies also commemorated Nazis who had died for the cause and a 'sacred fire' would be lit and a minute's silence observed by the assembled throng. Banners and swords were lowered as Hitler walked the length of the stadium. Legend has it that the Führer carried Longinus' spearhead with him at one of these events – just as so many of the previous owners had done at their moments of greatest triumph – but there are no photographs or any documentary evidence to support this story.

At probably the most notorious of these congresses in 1935, Hitler announced his infamous decree against German Jews that would make the future a living hell for these people. They were stripped of their citizenship, barred from the leading professions, and the already existing veto on marriage or sexual relations between Jews and Aryans was made a law. The even more spectacular rally in Nuremberg in 1937 when the names of over 400 dead Nazis were read out to the still and silent multitude were the first rumblings of the war that would very soon sweep across Europe.

Nuremberg had not, though, only become a shrine to Nazism. To its unique historical traditions, the new masters of Germany had added all the elements that made it a great industrial centre, too – confident as they were that its position in the east of the country in Bavaria was beyond the reach of any enemy attack.

The great castle at the centre of the city that somehow symbolised this dual might had been erected in 1050. By the Middle Ages, the community of outstanding buildings and fine churches that had grown up around it and along the banks of the River Regnitz, had attained importance as a commercial and cultural centre. The sixteenth century saw the city at the heart of the German Renaissance: famous as the birthplace of Albrecht Dürer, Hans Sachs, Peter Vischer and Michael Wolgemut, as well as a gathering-place for the Meistersingers, a centre for printing and the manufacture of the first pocket watches.

However, Nuremberg's status declined after the Thirty Years War, with up to 40,000 of its citizens dying as a result of starvation and other effects of the conflict. The next phase in the city's development did not occur until 1806 – initiated by Napoleon who, of course, knew all about the legendary holy spear. After defeating Prussia and Austria in 1806, he rewarded his ally, Bavaria, with the cities of Bamberg, Würzburg, Ansbach and Nuremberg. This reduced the once great walled city to part of a mere province.

Thankfully, the arrival of the industrial revolution

started the change in Nuremberg's fortunes. In 1835, the first steam railway in Germany was opened between Nuremberg and Fürth, followed shortly afterwards by the creation of the Germanic National Museum to gather together artefacts representing the nation's greatness. During the nineteenth century, the city also became a favourite with those who advocated Pan-Germanism and a symbol of all that was to be admired in the country' s culture – as typified by Wagner in *The Master Singers*, which he composed as a tribute to Nuremberg.

A century later, though, it was the turn of the Nazis to change the city's reputation to one of infamy as they developed their evil creed and harnessed its industrial heritage to further their military ambitions. The pioneer railway line became the hub of a vast system of rail yards, alongside which were built various huge factories, including the Siemens–Schuckert electrical works and the M.A.N. mechanical plant. Thereafter, until 1945, Nuremberg would be responsible for generating roughly half of the total German production of aeroplane, submarine and tank engines.

Almost at a stroke, Hitler had turned the cultural gem into a military powerhouse. And in so doing he had made the ancient and beautiful city for the first time in many years a legitimate target for enemy attack.

In February 1942 a special directive was sent to RAF Bomber Command in London from Winston

Churchill's War Cabinet. In future, it said, the primary objective of all night operations over Germany was to be 'focused on the morale of the enemy civil population and in particular the industrial workers'.

To help carry out this mission, a new chief marshal, Sir Arthur Harris, was appointed and the Command's older night bombers such as the Whitleys, Hampdens and Manchester's were phased out and replaced by Lancasters, Halifaxs, Wellingtons and Hamdens with their heavier bomb loads. These aircraft were also fitted with the newly designed Gee navigation system with its greater accuracy and ability to fix targets at ranges of up to 400 miles from England and at heights of 20,000 feet.

The Rühr, the Rhineland and the North German ports were the first to feel the effect of these new development, along with Harris' decision to concentrate his bombers on one target at a time and to make incendiary bombs an important part of every aircraft's payload. The greater accuracy with which the RAF navigators found their destinations enabled the pilots to unleash their bombs to much better effect – causing acres of the towns and cities to be laid waste by fire as well as considerably increasing the number of buildings destroyed or seriously damaged.

In the spring of 1942, Bomber Command carried out very successful raids on Essen – the site of the giant Krupps armament factories – Cologne and Bremen which despite the best efforts of the German defences to jam the Gee navigational device and shoot down the bombers, confirmed the effectiveness of Bomber Command and turned 'Bomber' Harris into a national hero. On 17 August of that year, the famous 'Pathfinder Force' was formed with four squadrons, all armed with 4,000-lb bombs curiously nicknamed 'Pink Pansies'.

It was a hail of these deadly weapons augmented by 250-pound incendiaries that fell from the night sky on to Nuremberg during the Pathfinder's fourth mission on the night of 28 August. The three earlier sorties – to Flensburg on the Baltic Sea, Frankfurt and Kassel had all been dogged by poor visibility – but the crews of the 159 Wellingtons and Hamdens had the benefit of a full moon for a visual sighting of the unmistakable walled city as they flew in towards it across the flat Bavarian countryside.

Even while the inhabitants were still rubbing sleep from their eyes, the anti-aircraft posts in and around the city opened up a blistering attack. A later report would state that twenty-three bombers were shot down, although at least fifty successfully released their bomb loads. The remainder of the flight dropped their explosives and incendiaries on the town of Erlangen, some ten miles to the north.

What is beyond doubt is that the raid inflicted most damage in the area around the ancient hall of St Katherine's church close to the city centre. It was here since the middle Ages that the Meistersingers had sung their famous 'Battle Songs' – which is probably one reason why it had seemed such an ideal place to Hitler for displaying the treasures of the *Reichkleinodien* including the spearhead of Longinus'. That and the long association of the treasures with the city.

Originally built in the thirteenth century as a convent, the hall had by this stage of the war come to be regarded by many visitors as more like a museum of Nazi trophies than a sanctuary for classic German music. Display cases of all shapes and sizes lined the walls and stood in serried ranks under the high, arched ceiling.

It was just after midnight when the bombs from the RAF planes fell on Nuremberg. The roof of the hall was damaged in several places, timbers and plaster tumbling into the darkened room and smashing several of the glass units, including the one in which the holy spear lay. Only the fact no explosive or incendiary bomb actually hit the building prevented the precious relic from being destroyed.

A rumour persists among a handful of researchers into the legend of the spear that one of the pilots over Nuremberg that night had been given specific orders to bomb St Katherine's because the spearhead was known to be there and its loss would certainly undermine Hitler's belief in his destiny. The orders were said to have come from Churchill himself – though there is no written record of any such instructions being given.

Apologists for this theory claim that the Pathfinder pilot was a religious man and was unable to bring himself to bomb a church. Instead, he unleashed his deadly load in the vicinity of the river after sighting the Imperial Castle, inadvertently damaging the roof of the hall. Whether this is anything more than an apocryphal story – as seems most likely – the castle was to feature very prominently in the next episode of the spear's journey through history.

In Max Caulfield's version of the legend, Hitler followed the example of previous owners of the spear by keeping it by his side during the first phases of the Second World War. As one victory followed another, he must have had good reason for acknowledging its powers. But, as the Irish author revealed in the second part of his enquiry, the Führer apparently underwent a dramatic change of heart – as indeed he was to do on numerous occasions during his ill-fated attempt at world domination. Caulfield writes:

Then something about the brooding, sombre strength of the spear's aura began to upset this volatile monster. His deep raking into the blackness of anti-Godliness may have been the cause. Certainly – and this is historical fact – he ordered the Lance of Longinus to be banished to the Nazi war treasures in Nuremberg. It was conveyed there in an armoured SS train under special guard. But the spear was not to be so easily shut out of its master's destiny. Exiled, it no longer caught the Führer's attention – but in moments of crisis, his thoughts were drawn back to it.

The information that Max Caulfield subsequently gathered – and which Trevor Ravenscroft and others including Francis King and J.H. Brennan have since augmented – makes it possible to trace what happened to the spear after the bombing of the hall of St Katherine's church on 29 August 1942.

When Hitler had made the decision that the spear and the other items of the *Reichkleinodien* were to be transferred to Nuremberg, he chose one of the Nazi Party's most long serving and devoted members to take charge and guard them with his life. Willi Liebel, a heavily built, dark-featured man, born in Nuremberg, who had joined the National Socialist Party not long after its inception, was chosen for this honour as a reward for his years of dedication to the cause. Not only had Hitler presented him with the original manuscript of his 'Nuremberg Laws' speech, but in 1939 had supported his appointment as *Oberburgermeister* of the city. Thereafter, Liebel's single-minded efforts on behalf of his Führer were boundless.

The morning after the Bomber Command night raid on his city, Burgomaster Liebel's first concern was not for those men, women and children who had been killed or injured in the raid – not even for the devastated property throughout the heart of the city – but to ensure that Hitler's precious treasure was safe. On seeing the shattered roof of the church hall he gave orders that the lance and the other precious items were to be removed immediately for safekeeping. Liebel was too terrified of Hitler's rage if anything happened to the items and had them sealed in a large box and taken to the nearby Kohn's Bank at 26, Königstrasse. Here the container was placed into one of the deepest vaults with strict instructions to the manager that it was not to be opened on any authority except his own.

There the spearhead remained until the following spring when another crucial event in the Second World War caused Hitler to have another change of heart – the German defeat at Stalingrad in February 1943. For the first time, the Führer had to contend with the thought that the soldiers of the mighty Third Reich might not be unbeatable. With the Russians poised to counter-attack against his Eastern Front and the British and their Allies using their aircraft to pound the western boundaries of his empire, security had become a top issue in all his plans.

Despite everything that clamoured for Hitler's attention that spring, he did not forget the spear. In April 1943, he gave orders that a permanent hiding place should be found for the *Reichkleinodien*. Whether he was suspicious of a bank with the name of Kohn can only be a matter for conjecture, but Heinrich Himmler, the Reichsfuhrer SS, was given orders to personally liase with Liebel to find a secure hiding place.

The evidence suggests that the Burgomaster

8 Diagram of the broken spear from
Die Reichskleindien in der Pfalz, 1942

proposed a number of locations in and around
Nuremberg. But one place apparently appealed more to
Hitler than any other – it just seemed so appropriate.
The spot was a tunnel some 900 feet below Nuremberg
castle, the fortress that had been reshaped and expanded
by his hero, Friedrich Barbarossa. The location was also
where legend had it that the Spear of Longinus had
been hidden once before in 1796 to avoid it falling into
the hands of the invading forces of Napoleon.

The castle had long been regarded as one of the most
important in the history of the German empire. From
1050 to 1571 all the German and Holy Roman emperors
had lived there, contributing at various times to its three

major sections: the *Kaiserberg* (emperor's castle) on the western side, the *Burggrafenveste* (count's castle) in the middle, and the oldest part, the *Stadburg*, to the east. A stone wall guarded by forty-six fortified towers and a moat had prevented the city from ever being sacked. Among these fortifications was the grim torture tower where some of the darkest events in the castle's history had occurred. It was where the 'Iron Maiden' was kept, too, a machine of appalling cruelty immortalised by Bram Stoker in 'The Squaw', a story almost as bloodthirsty as his classic novel of terror, *Dracula*.

Nuremberg castle had been built on sandstone, and according to historic records dating back to the fourteenth century, the hill beneath it was riddled with cavernous vaults and passageways. Despite suggestions to the contrary, these subterranean chambers that run over an area of 25,000 square metres, are not natural caves, but have actually been laboriously excavated by hand out of the rock. Because of their constant cool temperatures, they have proved ideal for the storage of all manner of things from beer to precious *objets d'art*. Ventilation shafts built hundreds of years ago also meant that securing the spear and the other holy relics there could be achieved with a minimum of people and delay.

Once a suitable tunnel had been picked, Liebel recruited two of his most trusted aides to move the treasure: Heinz Schmeissner, one of the city council's building experts, and Dr Konrad Freis, a specialist on air raid precautions. Conveniently, an entrance to the tunnel opened up on to the *Oberen Schmied Gasse* (Upper Blacksmith's Alley), a narrow row of picturesque houses backing on to the towering fosse on which the castle stood The doors of a garage adjacent to a seventeenth century gabled house in the alley provided an ideal front behind which steel doors were erected to conceal the tunnel entrance.

Under Liebel's hawk-eyed supervision, the tunnel was extended to 900 feet long and the passage widened. At the far end, air-conditioning was installed so that the precious artefacts would not be damaged by any dampness. When the job was done, Schmeissner and Freis were separately given a key to the vault door and a coding device that would only open the entrance when used together. Only the Burgomaster was in possession of duplicates of *both*.

Liebel was equally cunning when it came to moving the spear from Kohn's Bank to its new hiding place. The transfer was made late one night and the driver of the truck carrying the sealed container was ordered to take a long detour to Upper Blacksmith' s Alley so that the bank manager who had, of necessity, been present when the treasures were removed, had no idea of their destination. Liebel had also said nothing to Schmeissner and Freis about the spearhead's special significance to their Führer.

There, indeed, the Spear of Longinus remained safe until the night of 13 October 1944 when another devastating raid by Bomber Command on Nuremberg literally blasted the secret hiding place into the open. The RAF mission was by far the heaviest on the city and left whole districts in smouldering ruins. Once again, a number of the bombs fell in the vicinity of where the spear was hidden, blitzing several of the buildings in Upper Blacksmith's Alley.

As dawn broke the following morning, Willi Liebel received reports of where the enemy bombs and incendiaries had fallen. His heart stopped for a moment when he read of the devastation in *Oberen Schmied Gasse*. Without waiting to finish the reports, he hurried to the ancient street where his worst fears were immediately confirmed. The innocent-looking outer garage doors had been blown away and the steels doors revealed for all the world to see.

Liebel at once ordered workmen to the street. But his obvious anxiety to repair a locality that was hardly vital when compared with much of the other real carnage in the city soon began inciting rumours about the steel doors and effectively blowing the cover so carefully constructed for the treasures. As soon as word of this disaster was relayed to Berlin, orders were almost instantly returned to find another hiding place.

Obviously it was impossible to contemplate moving the relics from Nuremberg at such a dangerous period of the war and so another location in the town was necessary. One of Leibel's earlier ingenious suggestions, the basement of a school on the Panier Platz, opposite the entrance of the Upper Blacksmith's Alley, seemed ideal –

and perhaps less likely to arouse suspicion. The school had also been built into the sandstone beneath the castle and from the basement a concealed door opened into a labyrinth of passageways and caves.

A cave with a niche in the ceiling large enough to contain the *Reichkleinodien* was duly selected. The spear and the relics were then again re-sealed – this time in several copper containers – and cemented into the opening under the watchful gaze of Leibel, Schmeissner and Freis. The two assistants were never to forget just how anxious and drawn the normally blustering and arrogant Burgomaster was that morning in the gloomy basement beneath the Panier Platz.

Events in the Second World War – and the history of the spearhead – moved quickly after its concealment beneath the Nuremberg primary school. By the spring of 1945, the Allies and the Russians had retaken much of Hitler's doomed Thousand Year Reich and were already inside the borders of the Fatherland. By the end of March, the battered people of Nuremberg were trying to digest the information that American tanks and infantry had swept through Frankfurt and were now at Gemunden, just seventy-five miles away, with their city as an obvious target. Was this to be the first time in history when their fabled walls would fall to an invader?

Those living in the 'Spiritual Home of Nazism' did not have to wait long for the answer. Historical records show that the battle for the city began on 16 April with the arrival of the American 7th Army intent on breaking what had now become the last line of German resistance in the west with a pincer movement to surround Nuremberg. Defending the city were just twenty-two artillery regiments and a hundred Panzer tanks.

In a desperate appeal to the patriotism of his soldiers, Hitler sent a message to the embattled *Gauleiter* Karl Holz – 'Defend Nuremberg to your last drop of blood.' Whether or not he feared for the safety of his precious lance as he did for his people will never be known – but the remarkable response he got from the troops and, ultimately, the inhabitants of the city, to defy the Americans, turned the battle into one of the fiercest engagements of the war.

While Allied aircraft bombed the city from the air, an artillery barrage bombarded it constantly from outside the walls. Once inside the city, the 7th Army had to take it street by street. Graphic accounts of the conflict reveal that the toughest fighting occurred around the Congress Hall where Nazism had been born and was fanatically defended by detachments of the SS. Winning this last battle took a total of nine assaults by the veteran US 45th 'Thunderbird' Division who paid a high price in casualties.

Four days after the fighting had started, the ancient city of Nuremberg lay in almost total ruin, sacked for the very first time in its 900-year history. On 20 April the American flag was raised over Adolf Hitler Platz and, for those inhabitants who had survived, the nightmare was over. For Hitler, 250 miles away in Berlin, taking a glass of champagne to celebrate his fifty-sixth birthday, it was just beginning in earnest.

As Max Caulfield has reported, despite all his other preoccupations, the Führer never forgot the Spear of Longinus. As the inevitable stared him in the face, he took one further action to affect its already long and tangled history:

Just before his death, Adolf Hitler ordered the spear of destiny to be preserved. Three weeks from the end of his empire, the Führer laid his plans for the underground disappearance and future renaissance of his Nazi Party. He sent direct, personal orders to the Burgomaster of Nuremberg: 'Bury the spear in secret.' His wish was to bring it to light on the triumphal return to power, which he was already planning. Hitler, the invincible, could not see any other prospect.

So the Burgomaster of the city carried out Hitler's wish and the sacred lance was secreted away in a deep pit under the ancient castle. As the American troops poured into the city, the Führer committed suicide; and the secret of where the spear lay should have died with him. It is curious that it did not.

Curious is indeed a very apt word to have chosen for what *actually* occurred – for there are several versions of the events.

According to Caulfield, an unnamed official of the city council who was also a very religious man, grew uneasy about the fate of the spear. He feared about the effect on Christianity of the loss of one of its most holy relics and decided to tell one of the American commanders in the city where it lay. Within hours, a working party of GIs had unearthed the spear and brought it to their commanding officer. Caulfield goes on:

The C.O. was a rugged soldier who had fought long and hard. His war-tired eyes saw the incongruous, faintly pathetic remains on his desk and something about it stirred him deeply. Unconsciously, he felt a strange surge of power. He was the new – if only temporary possessor – of the spear of destiny The German who had led him to its hiding place had told him the legendary fable of its invincibility. 'Take it away,' he said quietly. 'Have a guard put on this thing – night and day.'

In a bunker under the war-torn city of Berlin at this moment, Adolf Hitler was abandoning his escape plans. For some reason his mind had suddenly changed. Was it mere coincidence? A few hours after the spear of invincibility passed out of his possession he pulled the trigger that ended his life.

This colourful finale to Max Caulfield's first account of the story of the spear is certainly intriguing and not without a certain degree of accuracy, as later research has established. The Burgomaster, Willi Liebel, certainly *did* commit suicide. The spear *was* rediscovered by the American occupiers. But the claim that Hitler killed himself when the spear was taken out of his possession is no more than coincidence.

The initial enquiries the Americans made as to the whereabouts of Willi Liebel revealed that the once high-profile civic leader had not been seen in Nuremberg after the start of the American attack on 16 April. Then while a group of civilians who had been recruited to help bury the bodies of the dead were clearing out the Palmenhof, the local SS headquarters on the Jacobsplatz, a body with a single bullet wound to the head was found in the cellar. A ring on one of the corpse's fingers with the initials 'W L.' confirmed to a member of the burial party who had known the man that this was, indeed, the *Oberburgermeister*.

Among those Nazis whom the Americans arrested on entering the city was Colonel Karl Wolf, the commander of the SS. Under interrogation, he admitted that Leibel had come to the Palmenhof on 19 April to discuss the future of the encircled city. He was prepared to fight, he said, but had decided he would never allow himself to be taken alive. Liebel then left the room and, moments later, Wolf said, he heard the sound of a shot and rushed down to the cellar where he found his visitor dead on the floor. A revolver lay by his side.

With his death – as Caulfield said – went what appeared to be the last chance of discovering the whereabouts of the spear. Even when the Americans were able to track down a man who had been Liebel's secretary on the council, they were no nearer the truth. Albert Dreykorn, a small, frightened figure, maintained that all the Burgomaster's secret files relating to the *Reichkleinodien* had been destroyed in an air raid on 2 January 1945. Another folder containing some further notes was burned on Liebel's orders two months later.

It would take a stroke of good fortune, in fact, to lead to the recovery of the missing hoard, plus the dedicated investigations of a resourceful Californian, Lieutenant Walter Horn, an art historian in civilian life. Horn had been recruited to a special section of the US Army Intelligence Service set up in the spring of 1945 with the somewhat euphemistic title of 'Monuments, Fine Arts and Archives' (MFAA). The unit's task under its commander, Captain Walter Thompson, was the tracing of all the treasures that had been looted by the Nazis during the war years.

Bomb damage once again provided a vital clue in helping to solve the mystery. On 30 April – by a very real coincidence, the day on which Hitler committed suicide in Berlin – a party of American soldiers sifting through the broken buildings and piles of rubble in Upper Blacksmith's Alley caught sight of the steel doors behind the gabled house that had again been exposed by bombing. The men could see at a glance that the doors must lead under the castle – which was by now serving as the 7th Army Headquarters. Ominously, there was evidence they had had been in use comparatively recently – though whether as a hiding place for Nazis or for storing loot was not immediately apparent.

When the discovery was reported to Colonel Charles H. Andrews, the Military Governor of Nuremberg, he was faced with a quandary. Should he blow open the doors and risk damaging whatever lay behind or try to discover a way of unlocking them? He chose the latter course and called in the Intelligence Service.

The case was handed to Lieutenant Horn who was already well briefed on the activities of Willi Liebel. Fortunately for the American, both Heinz Schmeissner and Dr Konrad Freis had survived the battle of Nuremberg and were still in the city. Their intimate knowledge of the workings of the community throughout the years of the war made them natural choices for interviewing.

The two men who, collectively, possessed the necessary information for opening the tunnel did not prevaricate long before revealing the coding system to Lieutenant Horn. Both also knew, of course, that the valuables that had so obsessed their former boss were no longer there and had been moved to the hiding place in the Panier Platz. But neither told Lieutenant Horn anything of this.

On 5 May, Schmeissner and Fries accompanied by

Colonel Andrews, Captain Thompson, Lieutenant Horn and a small clutch of army observers, opened the doors of the tunnel with the key and coded numbers. Inside the startled party came face to face with a king's ransom in Nazi loot: jewellery, paintings, relics and priceless antiques. But, as Horn soon discovered, there was no sign of the *Reichkleinodien*.

Although the two German city officials appeared as surprised as anyone else at the sheer magnitude of the hoard in the tunnel, they preserved their greater secret of the whereabouts of the Spear of Destiny. Only Lieutenant Horn observing the pair – in particular the shifty manner of Dr Fries – felt they knew more.

For the next three months, the persistent American questioned Schmeissner and Fries on a number of occasions, relentlessly picking holes in their stories. He also made several journeys across the shattered wastelands of Germany looking for clues and following up a number of quite extraordinary stories in the hope of solving the mystery.

These tales included a rumour that the hoard had been hidden at the bottom of Lake Zell in Austria. There was an even more remarkable claim that an elaborate decoy plan had been set up to give the impression that the spearhead and relics had been spirited away to another part of Germany, perhaps even *out* of the country – and maybe even to the ends of the earth . . . to Antarctica.

Nine

A Mystery in Antarctica

The deeply frozen stretch of Antarctica known Dronning Maud Land (Queen Maud Land) has been described as having 'more terra incognita' than anywhere else on the entire continent. It lies between 20°W and 45°E and resembles a vast desert of ice with several towering mountains and a number of deep crevices where no human foot has ever trod. The place represents in a phrase of the great explorer, Ernest Shackleton, 'one of the last great journeys left to man' – and very little has changed since he wrote these words over a century ago.

The reasons for Queen Maud Land being regarded as one of the most isolated areas of Antarctica – itself the coldest, stormiest, driest continent, covering an area of 14.2 million square miles and as such bigger than North America and Mexico combined – are not difficult to appreciate. With a surface layer of ice more than a mile thick in places, it is frequently battered by blizzards and torn by hurricanes that can reach speeds of up to 200 mph. The average 'summer' temperature in July is −63°C (−81°F) and the lowest temperatures can drop well below −70°C (−129F). For three and a half months there is no sunlight and like the rest of the continent, the territory is virtually sealed off from the rest of the world's weather systems.

Yet Droning Maud Land is also a place of otherworldly beauty. During the mid-year months, the sun never sets and just circles behind the mountains on the ice cap. Among the most striking of these edifices are the *Feriskjeftens* ('The Jaws of Fenris' after the fierce wolf of Norse legend), which rise from the snowy wastes like a row of flesh-eating teeth awaiting their victims. Equally forbidding is the *Rakekriven* − 'The Raven' − a towering shaft of granite over 2,000 feet tall. Sometimes, when it is especially cold, mirages known as *fata morgana* caused by temperature inversion can be seen dancing on the horizon.

Little, though, has been discovered about much of this landscape since the Russian, Thaddeus Bellingshausen, first sighted it while circumnavigating the continent in his ship, the *Vostok*, in January 1820. Apart, that is, from the obvious fact that it represents danger at almost every step. The evidence for this is probably nowhere more graphic than in the occasional finds of the mummified bodies of seals anywhere up to 100 miles from the coast − blown there by the wind, preserved by the arid, cold climate and perhaps centuries old.

The Norwegian, Roald Amundsen, the first man to reach the South Pole in December 1911, was also the first to explore Dronning Maud Land, naming it in honour of the country's beloved monarch, the daughter of Britain's Edward VII. He and his team discovered that despite the difficulty of living in the harsh and unyielding climate, its position facing the South Atlantic and its general inaccessibility still gave it considerable significance. One explorer told Amundsen with a wry smile that trying to find someone – or something – would be 'like looking for a needle in a haystack'...

The Germans have a long-standing fascination with Antarctica. Their explorers have been interested in the South Pole ever since 1874 when a *Kapitan* von Reibnitz led an expedition in his ship, the *Arkona*, to observe the phenomenon of the 'Transit of Venus' and established a small base on the Iles Kerguelen. The first German Polar Expedition was mounted a few years later in 1882, lead by Karl Schrader, and included an artist among the party, Eugen Mosthaff, who was responsible for making some of the first maps of the islands around the great ice-covered continent.

The first year of the twentieth century saw the arrival of the indefatigable explorer Erich Dogobert von Drygalski in his ship, the *Gauss*. He spent almost sixteen months observing the pack ice, making several journeys by sledge and a number of ascents in a tethered hydrogen balloon. This rose to 480 metres in altitude from where its occupants were able to relay information to the ship by telephone. An outbreak of illness, however, brought the expedition to a halt and it was left to the British explorer, Robert Scott, to carry out the first extensive exploration of Antarctica in 1902–3.

In 1911 the resourceful Wilhelm Filcher lead a well-prepared German South Polar Expedition with the intention of crossing the continent. Despite a successful start during which a new Ice Shelf was discovered and named after Filchner, the explorer' s ship, the *Deutschland*, became stuck in an ice pack for nine months. Although a winter sledge journey was able to disprove the American sealer Benjamin Morrell' s report of a 'New South Greenland' in 1823, the sudden death of the ship's captain, Richard Vahsel, caused the original plan to be reluctantly abandoned.

The defeat of Germany in the First World War forced the nation to renounce all it claims to sovereignty in the Antarctic under Article 118 of the Treaty of Versailles signed in June 1919. This was to prove just one of the many indignities that rankled Adolf Hitler and spurred his ambition to restore the glory of his nation – not just at home, but all over the world.

Hitler had evidently been fascinated by stories of polar exploration since his childhood. He had read accounts of the various German expeditions and developed what was to prove an abiding interest in life in the cold – indeed, he led a very chilly existence while living as an impoverished painter in Vienna. Even before he became Führer, in fact, he had formed a deep appreciation of the power of ice from the work of a man named Hans Horbiger and his theory of *Welteislehre* – 'The Doctrine of Eternal Ice'.

Like Hitler, Horbiger was an Austrian by birth, but he reaped such success as an engineer and designer of valve mechanisms, that he was able to retire when still a young man and devote all his energies to his theory. This had been developed from observing the moon through a telescope and deciding that it was probably made of ice. Horbiger conceived a perpetual struggle between fire and ice in the universe and in mankind that was outside the norms of conventional science. He believed the time was also right for a new world order. In his *magnum opus* entitled *Glacial Cosmogony*, published in 1913, he declared: 'Our Nordic ancestors grew strong in ice and snow; belief in World Ice is consequently the natural heritage of Nordic Man.'

Such beliefs fitted in precisely with Hitler's convictions, and he was later to refer to the author as 'the new Copernicus'. The evidence suggests that he not only read some of Horbiger's early pamphlets during his days in Vienna, but also the two men had several meetings before the author's death in 1931. True or not, there is little doubt that Hitler's thinking was deeply influenced by the 'World Ice Theory'. When in power, this became even more evident. He preferred, for example, the seclusion of snowy, mountain-top retreats for his command headquarters, like the famous 'Eagle's Nest' on the Obersalzberg Mountains and even adhered to Horbinger's theory when he came to make his crucial decision to invade Russia, as Pauwels and Bergier have written:

> In common with other disciples of the eternal ice theory, Hitler was firmly convinced that he had formed an alliance with the cold and that the snowy plains of Russia would not be able to delay his advance. Humanity under his leadership was about to enter the new cycle of fire. Winter would retreat before his flame-bearing legions.

Small wonder, then, that he cast covetous eyes over the polar territories and, especially, Antarctica, which consisted of 9.6 per cent of the world's land. He knew, too, that the continent was the only one with no owner or government, although several countries had claimed coastal sections.

According to Nigel Pennick, the Führer was thinking of Antarctica as being important to his plans for the future of Nazism as early as 1938. The vast wilderness would certainly be ideal as a refuge if the need ever arose – especially for the personnel, weaponry and means of finance that would insure his Thousand Year Reich against any eventuality. Later, it is claimed, he would see *Die Heilige Lanze* as essential to this plan.

The first Nazi expedition despatched by Hitler to explore Antarctica sailed from Bremen in the autumn of 1938. The ship, a large, meticulously equipped vessel, the *Schwabenland*, was captained by Alfred Kottas, a veteran of the South Atlantic seas, with Alfred Ritscher as the expedition leader. Their mission was to claim the deserted ice cap Dronning Maud Land for the Reich and rename it Neu Schwabenland.

According to the ship's log, Ritscher anchored off the coast early in January 1939 and remained there until the following month. Landing parties went ashore at Schirmacheroasen and other points along the coast, while two seaplanes, launched from the deck by steam catapult, flew over 350,000 km of territory between Kronprinsesse Martha Kyst and Prinsesse Astrid Kyst, photographing everything of interest. Aside from detailed pictures of the terrain, the aerial photographs also revealed for the first time another awesome mountain, 8,980 feet tall, which the explorers aptly named *Trollslotter* (The Troll Castle).

The Nazi pilots also dropped small Swastika flags over the frozen landscape to claim it for the Reich, as Pennick has written: 'Hitler's intentions were partly territorial, partly to further orthodox polar research and partly to corroborate Horbiger's claims. What became of the base, and its findings are shrouded in mystery. It is thought that a secret U-Boat base was established there.'

If we are to believe the story of U-Boat Captain

Otto Wermuth, then this is precisely what happened. And – according to him – it was to this base that Hitler's precious spearhead was secretly brought after the fall of the Third Reich.

There has, of course, been a great deal of discussion about the final days of Adolf Hitler in April 1945 and, in particular the manner of his death. Despite the constant reiteration by Otto Guensche, the Führer's last adjutant, that he had burnt the dictator's body 'to the last bone' with only a few teeth surviving the flames, rumours to the contrary have persisted ever since. In the immediate aftermath newspapers around the world carried stories with headlines that hinted at a dark secret. 'Is Hitler Really Dead?' the British *News Chronicle* asked, while *Paris-Presse* debated 'Hitler's Fake Suicide' and *The New York Times* added: 'Hitler Wed Actress in Berlin – May Be Alive in Europe'. The *Boston Globe* was even more specific: 'Hitler Sought In Boston' while Britain's sensationalist Sunday paper, *The People*, spoke confidently of 'Hitler's Argentine Connection'.

Hugh Trevor-Roper, one of the great historians of the Second World War and author of the classic work on the subject, *The Last Days of Adolf Hitler* (1945), which firmly ascribed the Führer's death in Berlin to suicide followed by the burning of his corpse, collected these reports assiduously. Five years later he wrote in the London *Daily Telegraph*:

In December 1946, a German aviator who called himself Baumgart testified in Warsaw that he flew Hitler and Eva Braun to Denmark on 28 April 1945. This story is pure invention. Despite the fact that Baumgart was subsequently committed to an institution, those who wish to believe him (and others) will certainly do so.

A story every bit as extraordinary as these – and perhaps just as questionable surrounds the spear at this precise moment in time. It claims that the holy relic was secretly transported by submarine to Antarctica and hidden in a specially prepared vault in a mountainous region of Queen Maud Land. The story has been recounted by a handful of newspapers, magazines and books from which I have drawn the following version of events.

Ever since Alfred Kottas had claimed Neu Schwabenland for Hitler in 1939, German ships had been busy in the waters around Antarctica. Not long after Britain entered the war, a merchantman, the *Schleswig-Holstein* was reported inspecting the coast, though there is no information that any of her crew landed before she was last seen heading in the direction of Cape Town. In 1940, a surface-raider, the *Atlantis*, used the seclusion of Antarctica to change her appearance to that of an innocent merchantman, the *Tamesis*, and thereafter sink a number of unsuspecting British vessels in the South Atlantic. The ship, complete with false wooden funnels and decks covered in packing cases to disguise her armament, was finally trapped and sunk by HMS *Devonshire*, near Ascension Island in November 1941.

Other suspicious German activities also went on around Queen Maud Land during the next four years of the war. A base code-named *Alstertor* was established to re-supply a group of Nazi raiders including the *Pinguin*, *Komet* and *Kassos*, which attacked and sank a number of British ships as well as several Norwegian whalers. In 1942, there were even full-scale plans for a meteorological station to be established, but after an extensive survey the order was countermanded.

Before the year was out, however, a Captain Gerlach in the raider, *Stier*, investigated a number of possible locations for a base for the commerce raiders and a camp to take prisoners-of-war. Members of his crew are believed to have spent several months on shore working on the project, before leaving as suddenly as they had arrived. No more reports of Germans in the waters off New Schwabenland are to be found until a mysterious visitor early the following year, described by Howard Buechner and Wilhelm Bernhart in their book, *Adolf Hitler and the Secrets of the Holy Lance* (1988):

In the spring of 1943, shortly after he replaced Admiral Erich Raeder as commander in chief of the German navy, Admiral Donitz dispatched a specially equipped submarine to Antarctica. This expedition built a large, steel reinforced entrance to a natural ice cave in the Muhlig-Hofman Mountains. The reason for this action has never been explained, except for the fact that Donitz was an unusually perceptive man and perhaps he had already envisioned the outcome of the war. At the very real end, Hitler named him as his successor as President of the Reich, an office which he actually held for a few days in early May, 1945.

Accounts of what supposedly happened at Neu Schwabenland when this ice vault was put to use have been gathered from the report of an anonymous Associated Press correspondent in Argentina, along with details supplied by the Scottish novelist, Duncan Kyle, author of *Black Camelot* (1978), and A.V. Sellwood, an English journalist who, in the immediate aftermath of the war, obtained unique access to several of the German seamen who had sailed the far reaches of the South Atlantic and turned their experiences into a best-selling book, *Atlantis: The Story of a German Surface Raider* (1955).

The mystery begins on 13 March 1945 when U-Boat 530, which had been on duty in the Baltic Sea, was urgently summoned back to its home port of Kiel for a new assignment. The sleek Type IXC/40 boat built by Deutsche Werft AG, Hamburg, had been commissioned in October 1942 and already carried out two successful years of operations in action under the command of *Kapitan* Kurt Lange. He had sunk over 12,000 tons of shipping before handing the boat over to its new commander, twenty-five-year-old *Oberleutnant* Otto Wermuth, in January 1945.

Wermuth, a dedicated Nazi, had just finished testing the U-Boat to its limits in the dangerous waters off the northern coastlines of Germany and Russia. He had pushed the engines to their maximum speed of 19 knots on the surface and 7.3 knots when submerged and taken himself and his crew near to U-530's maximum depth of 230 metres (755 feet). Because his mission had been cut short, the *Oberleutnant* had no opportunity to fire his 105/45 deck gun and had only used four of his torpedoes while cruising off the Norwegian coast.

As the young captain turned his vessel east and headed for home, he knew things were going badly for the Fatherland and probably wondered apprehensively what his new mission might involve. He did not have to wait long when he reached Kiel to find out.

Almost as soon as Captain Wermuth had clambered from the conning tower of U-530, he was aware of navy engineers and technicians beginning to swarm all over the 76-metre-long boat, clearly with instructions to prepare her for a quick return to sea. An official-looking car flying a swastika on the bonnet was waiting for him at the dockside and within minutes he was being driven out of the harbour gates towards the centre of the city.

The ride to his moment of destiny took Wermuth just five minutes, according to Duncan Kyle, who later investigated the mystery of the submarine's last voyage. Arriving at the local headquarters of the *Kreigsmarine*, he was shown into an office and introduced to Colonel Maximilian Hartman, an imposing figure who had apparently just come from the Führer's supreme headquarters in Berlin. Hartmann had been a protege of Professor Karl Haushofer and an aide to Hitler's personal secretary, Martin Bormann. Because he knew the history of the spear and its importance to the Führer, he had been especially entrusted with this mission.

The Colonel wasted no time in showing Wermuth six bronze-covered boxes that stood on a table in a corner of the room. The cases contained a selection of the Führer's most treasured possessions, he said, including the *Die Heilige Lanz*, and they were to be taken to a secret hiding place to save them from the enemies of the Reich. Wermuth would not know the precise location of this place until he was safely at sea, Hartman told him, handing him a sealed envelope.

The rest of that day went by in a whirl for the young captain. He was taken back to his submarine in a covered van, in the rear of which rested the six boxes with their precious contents. Before nightfall, all of them were safely stowed on the refuelled and re-provisioned U-530, which quietly slipped anchor. Wermuth set course for the North Sea, and beyond that, the vast open expanse of the Atlantic Ocean.

Just off the Bay of Biscay, the *Kapitan* tore open the sealed envelope Colonel Hartmann had given him. It took him several minutes to digest its extraordinary instructions – for he was to proceed to Antarctica and a locality approximately 71 degrees, 30 minutes south by 14 degrees, 51 minutes west. To ensure the absolute safety of his cargo, he was to run deep by day and only surface at the night.

The voyage southwards through the Atlantic, around the tip of South America and past the Falkland Islands into the chilly waters of the Antarctic Circle passed without incident. Off the coast of Queen Maud Land, Wermuth announced to his crew that a party of sixteen men were to be put ashore to deposit the six cases in a hiding place that had been specially prepared. The *Kapitan* handpicked the youngest and fittest members of the submarine's crew and broke out the sleds, special polar clothing and ample provisions, which had been stowed on board in Kiel. At the last moment, he handed the leader of the group, one of his officers, Lieutenant Karl Heinz Lenz, a route map to the site in the Muhlig Hofmann Mountain Range.

According to Duncan Kyle, once the party were on the icy shore, U-530 submerged to await their return.

It been estimated the party would need a couple of weeks to find the hiding place, leave the crates, and get back to the coast. The story is that it was not until the twentieth day that the sixteen men finally returned and gave the pre-arranged signal to the submarine by exploding a depth charge. Some of them were in a bad way by then, apparently suffering from frost-bite, and all of them said it had been a nightmare burying Hitler's secret hoard.

Wasting no more time, *Kapitan* Otto Wermuth and his crew disappeared beneath the waves and were not heard of again for almost two months. It was a reporter with the Associated Press Agency who picked up the next strand of the story of U-530 and published the facts in a syndicated article that appeared in several newspapers around the world, including the *Los Angeles Times* from which this version is extracted:

The last voyage of the German submarine U-530 ended with her surprise appearance in the harbour of Mar del Plata, an Argentina seaport 250 miles south of Buenos Aires, at sunrise on July 10, 1945, nine weeks after the end of the war in Europe. The 100-ton vessel was immediately surrendered to the Argentine authorities. Her commander, Captain Otto Wermuth, wearing the Iron Cross, with his fellow officers and the remainder of the crew, numbering 54, were taken ashore and detained.

Naval attachés at the British and American embassies examined the submarine after she had been taken over by the Argentine sailors. The U-Boat's guns had been jettisoned before her surrender.

On July 17, the Argentine government issued a decree handing over the U-530 to the British and United States governments, together with the crew and all available information concerning her belated and mysterious surrender.

A.V. Sellwood, whose book about the German raider, *Atlantis*, was written in conjunction with Ulrich Mohr, one of the members of her crew, also became fascinated with the story of U-530. He says that Mohr told him there were a number of rumours among German seamen about secret missions to South America and the Antarctic during the final days of the war. One of these even suggested that the Führer had not died in Berlin, but escaped by ship to a hiding place somewhere deep in the southern hemisphere:

There were all sorts of tales about the fate of many of the Nazi personalities, Hitler included. The Argentines got so concerned about this that the Minister of Marines was asked to investigate whether any German politicians or military officers had escaped to their country. This included the U-530, but they said that no one had reached the Argentine coast from the submarine before her surrender.

This did nothing, though, to dispel the mystery surrounding the boat, says Sellwood, referring to the account of the voyage given by Captain Wermuth.

When she arrived at Mar del Plata, the submarine was short of fuel, but had more than enough food. If, as her captain stated, she had been on patrol for nearly five months, she must have been obtaining supplies from somewhere, or been hiding in a safe place for some time. Even after the surrender of the U-530, for weeks afterwards there were unconfirmed reports from South America about the sighting of one or more submarines near the mouth of the Rio de la Plata (River Plate) and of mysterious landings in rubber boats on the coast of Patagonia.

So *had* U-Boat 530 really hidden the Spear of Longinus in Antarctica? The American and British government officials who examined the boat found a number of anomalies in Captain Wermuth's story that his mission had been purely to attack Allied shipping in the South Atlantic. The logbook had clearly been altered and all the documents relating to the mission had evidently been destroyed. There was also no explanation as to why the vessel, running low on supplies, but plentifully supplied with drink and cigarettes, had remained so long at sea after the end of the war had been declared.

Tales that the submarine had been on a secret mission only gradually came to light some years later when a couple of the crew members admitted the boat had stopped off at Antarctica. Neither man had been in the landing party – and they had no idea what was in the six crates they were carrying, beyond a rumour that the contents were 'very valuable'. The submarine itself was transferred to the USA and subsequently used for tests. On 28 November 1947, U-530 was scuttled by a torpedo northeast of Cape Cod and sank to a watery grave where she still lies to this day.

The story has continued to attract the attention of investigators ever since. In 1972, Warren Smith wrote in *This Hollow Earth*, 'Believers in the hollow earth theory claim a fleet of Nazi submarines took Hitler and his henchmen to a Nazi base set up under the ice cap at the South Pole.'

Ten years later, Nigel Pennick was adding to the story of Neu Schwabenland:

Several years after the fall of the Third Reich, a military expedition under Admiral Byrd left the United States for that very territory. Reports of US aircraft losses baldly stated, 'destroyed by enemy action'. Perhaps this southernmost Nazi base was the final remaining outpost of the Third Reich? Byrd's now-famous flight where he is said to have entered uncharted territory, thought by some to be into the 'inner world' of the hollow earth, took place at this time. Perhaps he was following up Nazi research, for their interest in the Hollow Earth Theory is well known. Even if he did not enter uncharted lands, the garbled account of the 'hollow earth' trip may have originated in Nazi documents seized during the expedition.*

Is it feasible, then, that the Germans could have built a secret hideaway in the icy fastness of Queen Maud Land? Certainly, in March 1998 scientists announced that a huge cavern had been found near Vostok, the Russian base in Antarctica, and other similar amphitheatres might exist below the surface of the continent. Speaking to the world's press after the discovery were announced, one of the explorers, Richard Hoover, said, 'We've found some really bizarre things – things we have never seen before It's like going to another planet, there are living creatures there that inhabited the planet more than 30 million years ago.'

He made no mention of any signs of *human* activity, however – nor even the remotest possibility that a lost hoard of Nazi treasures, including an ancient spear, might be somewhere around

Back in Germany in the summer of 1945 the story of the holy lance and the other treasures being spirited out of the country by submarine, was one of only several rumours that the American Army Intelligence Service were busy investigating A report by the AIS at this time that is now filed in the Library of Congress in Washington under the

---

*The full story of the Nazi 's interest in the 'Hollow Earth Theory' and the enduring legend of an interior world inside our own is told is this author's book, *The Hollow Earth Enigma* by Alec MacLellan (Souvenir Press, 1999).

heading, 'Report on Recovery of Imperial German Insignia of Holy Roman Empire', indicates just who the instigators of two of these stories might have been:

It may be inferred that the idea of covering up the tracks of the removal by the fictitious story that the insignia had been sunk to the bottom of a lake [Lake Zell, near Salzburg] must have originated in the highest circles of the German Security Service [SS], and that the orders to stage a fake removal of the insignia from Nuremberg came from Berlin. The fact that not even the heads of the *Reichssicherheitshauptamt* were considered worthy of being initiated into the secret illustrates the political importance attached to it.

On the ground of these facts and conversations between captured SS officials, which were reported by the Third Army Intelligence Centre, it would appear that the Imperial Insignia were slated by the chiefs of the German Security Service to become the symbols of the future German resistance movement *Oberburgermeister* Liebel of Nuremberg may have been aware of this role of the Insignia. The other city officials who participated in their removal were not.

The persistent Lieutenant Walter Horn was, however, far from sure that Dr Freis and Heinz Schmeissner were not holding back information, though both persisted in telling the same story. They claimed that a convoy of SS

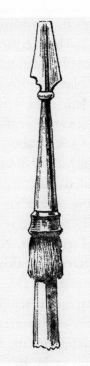

9 Undated sketch of the spear from the American Army
Intelligence Service files in the Library of Congress

men had arrived on the morning of 2 April in Upper
Blacksmith's Alley. There, under the anxious gaze of
Willi Leibel, the tunnel behind the old house had been
opened and the *Reichkleinodien* loaded into wooden
boxes and driven away. Their stories were, as Horn
knew, a repeat in almost every respect of the rumour
that the treasure was now at the bottom of Lake Zell.

The lieutenant was just not convinced. Then, a chance
meeting with an old friend working for the US Field

Intelligence in Munich provided him with further confirmation that he had been right to be suspicious. Jack Rosenthal was responsible for installing listening devices in the cells of former Nazis to record their conversations. When Horn asked him if he could help him in his particular mission, Rosenthal replied that he 'distinctly remembered two men talking about the "Crown Jewels" that were buried in the hill at Nuremberg'.

Rosenthal provided his friend with detailed information from the conversations that had been 'bugged' and also a list of some very interesting names that had emerged. Lieutenant Horn drove back to Nuremberg more determined than ever to wring the truth out of Dr Konrad Freis. On 3 August, after being arrested and locked up for the night in the Third Army's intimidating Theatre of Interrogation, the former expert on air raid precautions must have felt the world had fallen in on him, as Horn's report, also filed in Washington, reveals:

The investigation in Nuremberg having come to a deadlock, Lt Horn decided to confront *Stadtrat* (Town Councillor) Freis with *Oberführer* Spacil, then suspected of being the SS Officer to whom the Insignia had presumably been handed by *Oberburgermeister* Willi Liebel. Under the effects of a night of solitary confinement and the pressure of a short interrogation which preceded the scheduled confrontation, Freis broke down and confessed.

The broken man admitted that many of his previous statements had been false. The insignia had never been handed to anyone from the SS. He and Leibel had been responsible for encasing it in masonry in the underground bunker in the Panier Platz on 31 March. In order to cover up this removal, a fictitious operation had been staged on 2 April with the assistance of local SS men. Dr Freis was at last willing to reveal the location of the lost treasure and assist in its recovery.

Lieutenant Horn's report adds that after Schmeissner was confronted with Freis' statement he, too, confessed to his part in the episode. On the morning of 7 August, the two prisoners accompanied by Captain Thompson, Lieutenant Horn, an insignia expert, and two soldiers, a stone mason, all assembled at the entrance to the bunker in the Panier Platz. The statement concludes:

Fries and Schmeissner directed the party to the hiding place, a small room in the subterranean corridor system, approximately 80 feet below the surface of the Panier Platz. After a hole had been chiselled through the brick wall of one of the small ends of the room, the four copper containers, with the Insignia, were recovered. In the presence of all the persons who witnessed the recovery, the copper containers were transferred to their original place, the art cache underneath the Nuremberg Castle, where they are kept behind steel doors.

The *Reichkleinodien* was to remain in Nuremberg for another five months while the wheels of bureaucracy turned slowly to obtain permission for the ancient treasures to be returned to the Austrian Government. This was not, though, without a protest from Dr Ernst Gunter Troche, the director of the Germanic National Museum – which, remarkably, had survived the worst of the Allied onslaught – who claimed that the insignia belonged in Nuremberg. The German people, he said, 'have a common interest and right for such a solution'; while the city itself 'has a historical right to be trustee of the regalia'. Nonetheless, General Dwight Eisenhower, the Supreme Commander of Allied Forces in Europe, denied the request and ruled that all the treasure should go back to Vienna where Hitler had unlawfully seized it.

On 4 January 1946, the precious hoard was taken from the ruins of what had been the 'Spiritual Home of Nazism' and flown in an American Dakota from Furth Airport to Vienna. There, on 6 January and without any ceremony, General Mark Clark quietly handed it back to the city.

A month later, the holy relics were once again on display in the Schatzkammer. But with the spear's reappearance after its years in the hands of Adolf Hitler a greater mystery arose. Was it the *real* one? Or might it just be a *duplicate* that had been cleverly substituted in the panic and confusion of the last days of the Third Reich? The answers to the questions – when they were forthcoming – were once again not without more surprises.

Information collected since the end of the Second World War indicates that there were, in fact, *three* relics listed as 'holy spears' in Germany between 1938 and 1945. One was the 'Spear of Longinus' seized by Hitler in Vienna. The second was a brilliant copy made especially for Heinrich Himmler, the most notorious of the German leaders after Hitler. And the third, 'The Maurice Lance', which is the centre of a bizarre controversy.

Himmler, the *Reichsführer* SS, was one of the earliest members of the Nazi party. He was privy to the secret life and obsessions of the Führer and shared his fascination with the occult. In fact, he had been casually interested in the subject since his youth, but this became a driving force in 1928 when he married Margarete Boden, a Prussian landowner's daughter who dabbled in mesmerism, cosmology and herbalism. Under her influence, Himmler, a lapsed Catholic, was soon investigating witchcraft and formulating a theory that the persecution of witches in the seventeenth century represented a kind of holocaust of the German race that had been carried out by the Roman Catholic Church. 'The witch-hunting cost the German people hundreds of thousands of mothers and women, cruelly tortured and executed,' he was later quoted as saying.

The SS leader ultimately assembled a collection of

over 140,000 books on witchcraft and used his authority to have members of his staff compile an index of 34,846 cases of executions for witchcraft in Germany and around the world to support his theory and justify a terrible revenge. Himmler's researches also made him a convinced believer in reincarnation, a fact confirmed in a speech given to high ranking SS officers at Dachau in 1936 and reported by Francis King:

He believed that he himself was the reincarnation of Heinrich the Fowler, the monarch who had founded the Saxon royal house, had driven the Poles eastward and whose memory he held in peculiar veneration. On the thousandth anniversary of Heinrich's death he swore an oath to continue the king's 'civilising mission in the east' and each year thereafter he spent some time in silent meditation before the dead monarch's tomb which, so he said, was 'a sacred spot to which we Germans should make pilgrimage.'

Heinrich the Fowler had, of course, been the proud owner of the Spear of Longinus during his lifetime and Trevor Ravenscroft believed that the relic also became one of the abiding obsessions of the *Reichsführer's* life:

Whereas Adolf Hitler waited patiently for thirty years between his first sight of the spear in the Hofburg and the day he claimed it as his own possession, Heinrich Himmler anticipated the event by having an exact replica of the Spear made for himself in 1935, three years before the Führer annexed Austria and plundered the treasures of the Habsburg Dynasty. It was a threat contained within a Germanic prophecy made a thousand years ago that spurred Himmler to order a replica of the Spear associated with a legend of world destiny. This prophecy, from the lips of a Saxon soothsayer in the tenth century reign of King Henry the Fowler, spoke of a 'gigantic storm that would appear out of the East to overwhelm the German peoples if it was not confronted and turned back in the region of Birkenwald in Westphalia.'

Himmler's replica was given pride of place in the Wewelsburg, an ancient castle situated near the town of Paderborn in Westphalia, which became known as the 'physical centre of his SS paganism'. He purchased the building in 1934 in a ruinous state and set about turning it into a fortress capable of withstanding the 'forces from the east' the old legend had predicted. In the years to 1945, Himmler is reputed to have spent 13 million marks on magnificently refurbishing the granite pile. He also dedicated its finest rooms to various legendary German heroes, including Otto the Great, Henry IV and Frederick Barbarossa – all, of course, previous owners of the spear.

The duplicate lance – which one story claims was made, unknown to Himmler, by a highly skilled Jewish jewellery maker, while another version maintains it was actually an antique found in the old Roman city of Trier in Germany that had been expertly renovated – stood on the *Reichführer*'s desk in an antique wooden box. He gave instructions that it was to remain there, resting on a richly embroidered red cushion, until Hitler reclaimed the original from Austria. Then he was confident it would be given to him as a symbol of the new order. Himmler's disappointment when this hope failed to materialise can only be imagined – although there is no argument about the wrath he subsequently directed against all religions that disputed the creed of Nazism.

It was in 1945 when the Third Reich was in its dying days that the paths of Himmler's replica and the third relic known as 'The Maurice Lance' crossed. The facts about this curious episode are to be found in the writings of Duncan Kyle, Trevor Ravenscoft, Howard Buechner and Wilhelm Bernhart. First, Duncan Kyle writing in *Black Camelot*, says:

On March 31, 1945, a group of SS engineers under the command of Major Heinz Macher attempted to destroy Wewelsburg Castle on the orders of Himmler himself. Two days earlier, the duplicate Holy Lance had been secretly removed and sent to Nuremberg for safekeeping with other treasures of the Reich.

The treasure was, of course, the *Reichkleinodien*, hidden by the burgomaster, Willi Liebel, and shortly to emerge into the light of day once again. Before this happened, however, an 'extraordinary and comical misunderstanding' took place, according to Ravenscroft, that would ensure the legend of the Spear of Destiny changing owners would continue.

> When Liebel enumerated the items to be hidden in an alternative hiding place he called the Holy Lance, 'The Maurice Lance'. It so happened that one of the six central pieces of the treasure was a sword known as 'The Maurice Sword'. And it was the sword of St Maurice which was hidden instead of the lance of St Maurice.'

It was this confusion – Buechner and Bernhart claim in their book, *Adolf Hitler and the Secrets of the Lance* – that resulted in an even more bizarre twist to the story: 'When the cache in Nuremberg was uncovered on April 30, 1945, the real lance was in, or en route to, Antarctica and Himmler's imitation spear had taken its place in the Reich collection.'

The scientific tests in Vienna in 2003 have, of course, proved that the spear in the Schafzkammer' in Vienna is no twentieth-century fake. But even this ancient relic is not old enough to have pierced the side of Christ. So where – amidst all this mixture of myth and rumour – is the real spear, if it still exists at all. The answer lies some thousands of miles away from Antarctica, Europe or even the Middle East – in the fastness of Asia Minor.

Ten

The Secret of Gheghardavank

There are sections of the ancient city of Kayseri, located deep in the windswept heartland of Turkey, that are almost biblical in appearance – which is perhaps not surprising as at the time of Christ it was an impressive Roman community known as Mazarca. Situated at the foot of the hulking, snow-capped Erciyes Dagi – a 3,916-metre-high extinct volcano, the ancient Mount Argaeus – the city has been in existence for 6,000 years and in classical times was the capital of Cappadocia. Kayseri is, in fact, full of imposing reminders of the past . . . and one vital clue to the whereabouts of the true Spear of Longinus.

The city first became important during the years of the Hittite empire, primarily because it stands at the junction where the main trade routes leading east from the Aegean coast cross those going north and south between the Mediterranean and the Black Sea. For years the state of Cappadocia was fiercely independent – and then the Roman legions arrived. The last puppet king, Archelaus I (37BC–AD17), changed the name to

Caesarea in honour of his patron, Caesar Augustus. (The modern Kayseri is, in fact, only a slight derivation of the Roman name.)

However, Caesarea's exposed position on Turkey's central plateau made it a prime target for invading armies and it passed from the Romans to the Byzantines and later the Selcuks, Mongols, Mamelukes, until finally being annexed to the Ottoman Empire in 1515. The great, black volcanic stone *ic Kale*, or citadel, with its nineteen basalt towers that stands in the centre of the city, built by Emperor Justinian during the sixth century, is the most distinctive landmark and a vivid reminder of Kayseri's embattled past. Amidst the ancient mosques with their towering minarets and the elegant architectural buildings clustered in the busy streets, stands the impressive thirteenth century Doner Kumbet, which literally means 'revolving Tomb'. A twelve-sided, cone-roofed mausoleum it does not actually turn, but a local legend says that the pure of heart can see it slowly rotating very early in the morning.

The area around Kayseri is unparalleled in both history and mystery. As a result of eruptions from Mount Erciyes millions of years ago, the surrounding plateau was smothered in a soft stone made of lava, ash and mud which centuries of rain, wind and flooding have transformed into an otherworldly landscape of cone-shaped white monoliths known as *Peribaca* or 'fairy chimneys'. The inhabitants of this area have been of varying lineage, and while the Bible insists that the Mushki and Tabal tribes living in Cappadocia were the 'coarsest people on earth', other ancient writers have made particular mention of the unrivalled beauty of their women.

This astonishing region has also been a hotbed of religious activity for centuries. From about 525BC, the fire-worshipping Zoroastrians from Persia revered the volcanic Erciyes Dagi Mountain. Then the first Christians formed a stronghold in Cappadocia and by the fourth century, it had become a major centre for Christian teaching and philosophy. As Selin Tuysuzoglu writes in his guide to *Turkey* (2001): 'Hiding from Romans, Iconoclasts, Sassanids and Turks, these hardy Christians carved beautiful frescoed churches and colossal underground cities into the pliant tufa.'

Kayseri remained an important centre of Christianity until the Arab invasions of the seventh century. It became famous, too, as the birthplace of St Basil (the Great), acknowledged as one of the founding fathers of.the early Christian Church. Born in 329, he succeeded Eusebius as bishop of his native city and was responsible for organising the monastic life of Cappadocia as well as writing a series of important works about the Christian faith.

Long before this, however – over 300 years, in fact – there was another important early Christian who lived in Kayseri. Indeed, the fact of his existence there is the last definite piece of evidence known about his life. He

was Gaius Cassius Longinus, the Roman centurion
whose spear had pierced the side of Christ.

Today, there are four spearheads that have been claimed
as the lance used by Longinus at the Crucifixion. The
first, of course, is in Vienna. There is a second in the
Vatican in Rome; a third in the Polish city, Cracow; and
the most compelling claimant of all in Armenia. There
are also stories of a 'spear' that was found at Antioch –
the modern Antakya in Turkey – the ultimate fate of
which is surrounded in mystery.

The history of the spearhead in Rome is long and
tortuous. It begins in the year ad 570 when a pilgrim
named St Antoninus of Piacenza visited Jerusalem.
There, in the Basilica on Mount Sion he came face to
face with two remarkable relics, which he later
described in his *Breviarus*: 'There are many holy places
in Jerusalem and in the Holy Sepulchre I saw the crown
of thorns with which Our Lord was crowned. There
was also the lance with which He was struck in the
side.'

There are similar accounts of this spear being
venerated by pilgrims visiting Jerusalem in the writings
of the Calabrian scribe, Magnus Cassiodorus, and
following him by the sixth-century Frankish historian,
Gregory of Tours, in his hagiographical compilation,
Miraculorum Libre VII. However, in 615 when the city
was captured by the Persian King Chosroes, 'the sacred
relics of the Passion fell into the hands of pagans,'

according to a contemporary document, the *Chronicon Paschale*. This report continues:

> When the seizure took place, the point of the lance, which had been broken off, was given in the same year to King Nicetas, who took it to Constantinople and deposited it in the church of Hagia Sophia in Constantinople. There the point of the lance was set in a *yeona*, or icon.

The broken spear was not heard of again until 1244 when the tip of it was said to have come into the possession of Emperor Baldwin II of Constantinople. However, when an invading army of Greeks forced the emperor to flee the city in 1261, he presented it to Louis IX, the thirteenth-century crusader and King of France. The King then took the fragment to the Sainte-Chapelle in Paris where it remained until the outbreak of the French Revolution. During this period of upheaval, it seems, a number of holy relics were removed to the Bibliotheque Nationale for safekeeping. Unhappily, the metal splinter disappeared while there and has never been seen again.

The second and larger part of the broken lance enjoyed better fortune, however. About 670 it was seen safely back in the Holy Sepulchre in Jerusalem by the Roman historian, Arcuplus. He noted that the Byzantine emperor, Heraclius, had apparently done some restoration work in the interim to preserve the spear.

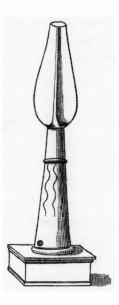

10a The holy spear of Rome

Heraclius, who had been born in Cappadocia, was a brilliant soldier and tactician, but is said to have wasted his glory in 'self-indulgence and theological disputes'. Later pilgrims to Constantinople, including the noted English traveller, Sir John Mandeville flocked to view the restored spear. Sir John, whose journeys took him through Europe, Turkey, Persia, Arabia, North Africa and India, claimed in his book of *Travels* to have seen both parts of the spear – the tip in Paris and the larger portion in Constantinople – in the year 1357, 'and the latter is much larger than the former'.

In 1492, Turks invading Constantinople seized the holy relic once again along with a great deal of other valuable treasures. According to Henry Pastor's *History of the Popes* (1889), the Ottoman Sultan Beyazid II decided to send the spear as a gift to Pope Innocent VIII to secure the release of his brother, Zizim, who was then the pontiff's prisoner. As soon as it arrived in Rome, the lance without its tip was given a place of honour in St Peter's Church. Just over a century later, in 1606, the spear became the centrepiece of a monument, the *Ciborium de la Sainte Lance*, designed by Francesco Grimaldi to honour Pope Innocent VIII.

Interestingly, at this time the first doubts were being expressed as to the authenticity of the relic because of the 'rivals' known to be in France and Germany, but no one – scholar or layman – appears to have examined the respective claims. This had to wait until the end of the nineteenth century when a French expert on religious artefacts, M.F. de Mely, carried out an extensive investigation into the spear in St Peter's. He published the results in what is now regarded as one of the definitive studies of the legend, *Exuviae Sacre Constantinopolitanae*, which appeared in Paris in 1904.

De Mely was able to obtain 'an exact drawing of the point of the lance from an old manuscript in the Ambroisienne in Milan' and compare this with the larger relic in Rome. He reported that he was satisfied, 'the two fragments had originally formed one blade'.

Today the larger spearhead rests between the four pillars surmounting the altar of St Peter's Basilica in the Vatican. The church also has a magnificent statue of St

Longinus by Gianlorenzo Bernini, showing the legionnaire with his arms raised in exhortation and the famous spear clutched in his right hand. In a brief statement issued to this writer, a spokesman of the Vatican said, 'The Catholic Church makes no claim as to its authenticity.'

The metropolis of Cracow which lies in a broad valley on the banks of the River Malopolska is the fourth largest city in Poland, although for centuries it was the nation's capital and rivalled in size and opulence other great central European cities like Budapest, Prague and Vienna. Most of its many ancient buildings and historical sites are situated in and around the medieval Old Town, the skyline of which is dominated by the twin towers of St Mary's Church in the Main Market Square. To the south, on a hill, lies the magnificent Wawel Castle, which overlooks the scenic 'Vistula Bend' where the river turns at almost ninety degrees.

There is, though, one building more strongly associated with the history of Cracow – and the whole history of Poland, for that matter – the magnificent Gothic cathedral. It is actually the third building to have occupied the site since the original foundation stone was laid in 1020. The existing Cathedral was built between 1320 and 1364 by King Wladyslaw to house the relics of St Stanislaw who was much venerated by the Poles. It contains numerous chapels, three towers and in the entranceway hangs the bones of an 'ancient creature'. According to legend, when they fall the world will come to an end.

The focus of interest as far as the legend of the spear is concerned is the cathedral treasury, an imposing building whose origins go back to the eleventh century. It is reached via the sacristy and by passing the extraordinary Crucifix of Queen Jadwiga. Tradition maintains that the queen – who was later declared a saint – used to pray in front of the very expressive fourteenth-century cross and relics of her now rest in the altar.

The treasury's unique collection of religious objects is not, however, open to the public – although a number of items including jewelled swords, gold and silver royal insignia, richly embroidered coronation robes and various church reliquaries and vessels have occasionally been put on display in the adjoining cathedral museum. One of the highlights of the collection – though it has rarely been seen – is a spearhead, the history of which has been encapsulated by the scholar M. Przezdziecki in his *Bibliotheca Warszawka* (1861), citing the ancient text of the *Miracula Sancti Adalberti Martiris*:

The spearhead has been kept in the Treasury for eight centuries. The legend says that it is the Lance of St Maurice given to Boleslas the Brave who was first duke and then king of Poland, by Otto III at the time of the pilgrimage made by the emperor to the tomb of Saint Adalbert in Gnese, Poland, in the year 1000. It was the sign of authority and it is thus that Charles Martel conquered the Saracens at Poitiers in 731 with the lance of Saint Maurice. It is likely that Otto III had the lance made in the style of the holy imperial lance in order to give it to his powerful ally Boleslas of Poland.

Historians are, however, puzzled by the mention of the warrior, Charles Martel, possessing the spear. Martel, 'The Hammer', who was born in 676, the son of Pepin of Heristal, is best remembered for winning the Battle of Poitiers, which has been romanticised as the salvation of Europe from the Arabs. A clever and ferocious fighter, he was chosen to be a duke by the Austrian Franks in 714 and within five years was their ruler. After a great deal of hard fighting with the Saxons, Alemanni and Bavarians, Charles' moment of destiny came when confronted by the tide of Moslem invaders which had swept through southern Asia, North Africa, the Iberian peninsula and much of southern France in a desperate battle fought over the countryside between Tours and Poitiers.

In one or two accounts of this savage conflict, Charles Martel is credited with leading his troops into battle brandishing the same lance that St Maurice had carried when defying the might of the Roman Empire. However, this story seems improbable as the very name Martel that has immortalised him ever since his death in

741 comes from the very weapon with which he always fought – an enormous hammer.

Martel's reputation was initially built on his innovation of adding stirrups to the saddles of heavy cavalry horses, which enabled his warriors to remain seated on their mounts. This invention – which came to be known as 'shock combat'– allowed the men to carry a heavy lance one-handed at the rest position while the stirrups kept them firmly in the saddle. The men were then free to impale an enemy on the lance, using the full momentum of their own weight as well as that of their charging horses.

The only problem with this innovation was that the victim was often struck with such force that he would become impaled on the end of the lance, leaving the warrior unable to defend himself in the fury of battle. Martel's armourers found a solution by adding a baffle arrangement near the tip of the lance to keep it from penetrating a victim too deeply. This new weapon was known as 'the winged lance' and provides the explanation that, I believe, makes Trevor Ravenscroft mistaken in his assertion in *The Spear of Destiny*:

> The mystical talisman [became] an actual weapon in the hands of the Frankish General Charles Martel (The Hammer) when he led his army to gain a miraculous victory over the massed forces of the Arabs at Poitiers (732AD). Defeat would have meant

that the whole of Western Europe would have succumbed to the rule and religion of Islam.

The Hammer that actually earned Martel his soubriquet was said to have been found by him either while out hunting in a wood, given to him by a wizard, or passed on by an ancestral god – the variations are almost infinite and most of them undoubtedly encouraged to spread by Charles in order to intimidate his enemies. The weapon itself was believed to be between three to four feet long with a massive head carved with strange runic patterns that endowed it with magical powers. The shaft was wooden and claimed to be fire-resistant. According to legend, Charles swung the hammer 'as if it were a mere sword', but no other man could even lift it. There is, unfortunately, no record of what ultimately happened to this extraordinary 'winged lance'.

The spear of Cracow, however, remains under lock and key in the treasury of Cracow cathedral. It may very well have been this secrecy that caused Hitler – for one – to declare it a fake in 1938 even though he never saw it. No doubt his intention was to enhance the authenticity of his own spear.

The photograph and sketch that I have been able to obtain – reproduced in this book – clearly show the Cracow Spear to be similar to the one in Vienna. Indeed, the historian, Friedrich Sprater, who sketched it half a century ago, referred to it unequivocally in his book, *Die Reichskleinodien in der Pfalz* (1942), as 'perhaps the best known of a number of inexact duplications of the true lance'. The church authorities of Cracow cathedral – like those in Rome – similarly make no claim as to its authenticity.

The next relic put forward as the Centurion's lance did not come to light until the time of the First Crusade in 1098 and is, in all probability, not a spear at all. The story behind it is another mixture of fact and fable and begins with the life of a humble monk named Peter Bartholomew at a moment in time when 100,000 starving and disease-ridden Crusaders faced almost certain death at the hands of more than a quarter of a million Turks.

The first of what would ultimately become a series of Crusades to reclaim the Holy Land – in particular Jerusalem and the Holy Sepulchre – from Islam during the eleventh to fourteenth centuries, began in France in 1095. At the Council of Clermont that year, Pope Urban II exhorted Christians throughout Europe to make war against the Infidels, promising that the arduous journey would count as a full penance for their sins and a truce would be put into effect to protect the property of anyone who went during the time they were away. It was from the crosses distributed at this gathering that the Crusaders took their name.

The First Crusade which set off that same year, consisted of several undisciplined hordes of French and

10b The sacred lance of Cracow

German peasants led by a charismatic preacher known as Walter the Penniless. This rabble started out by massacring Jews in the Rhineland and then outraged the Bulgarians and Hungarians with their debauchery and looting before they were driven off. By the time they reached Constantinople, the numbers of the 'Crusaders' had been severely reduced. The remnants crossed into Asia Minor, but were easily defeated by the Seljuk Turks.

In 1097, however, a properly organised army of Crusaders followed in their wake. They were led by Count Raymond IV of Toulouse and included Godfrey, Duke of Lower Lorraine, Bohemond I and his cousin, Tancred. Once in Turkey, the Europeans allied with the Byzantine emperor, Alexius I, and renewed the fight against the forces of Islam.

These better-equipped and organised Crusaders were soon at the walls of Antioch – the modem town of Antakya (Hatay) on Turkey's eastern Mediterranean coast – and at that moment in time the third largest city in the world after Rome and Alexandria. There they laid siege to the Turkish stronghold beside the River Orontes at the foot of Mount Sipylus and overran it.

For a while the Crusaders paused for rest and recuperation in the sprawling community that had been founded in 301BC by Seleucus and turned into a great trading centre, thanks to the routes criss-crossing from the Euphrates to Asia Minor. The men also became aware of Antioch's long history of violence – both man-made and natural – which had included several terrible earthquakes: notably one in AD526 when around 250,000 people had died. Because of its location, though, the city was difficult to defend and signs of previous attacks, sackings and burnings were still evident in the walls. (Interestingly, among the many finds made during later excavations in the area have been the 'Great Chalice of Antioch' claimed by some experts to be the Holy Grail.)

Within months of the arrival of the Crusaders, however, a large and well-supplied force of Turks returned to surround the walls of Antioch, seemingly prepared to lay siege for as long as it took to reclaim the town. The occupants of the city had the option of being killed or dying of starvation. It was at this moment of crisis – so the accounts have it – that a vision of the spear of Longinus changed everything.

It was on 10 June 1098 that Peter Bartholomew, a monk in the service of a member of Count Raymond's army and a man with something of a reputation as a mystic, went to see the leader of the Crusade. He was anxious to tell him and his spiritual adviser, Bishop Adhemar of Puy, about a series of dreams he had been experiencing. Richard Rainey provides the facts in *Phantom Forces* (1990):

> Peter Bartholomew could no longer hold back about the visions that had been coming to him ever since they had arrived at Antioch. St Andrew had appeared to him and commanded him to find the Lance of Longinus that waited for them beneath the ground. The Apostle had transported Peter inside the church, then lifted a lance from the ground, telling him it was the lance used by Longinus.

Although Count Raymond took the story seriously, Bishop Adhemar was sceptical. There the matter might well have ended, in fact, if rumours of the monk's vision had not spread throughout the besieged city. Within a matter of days, other Crusaders – including a priest – claimed to have had similar dreams. This time the word of the man of the church swayed Bishop Adhemar and he agreed that a dig in the church should take place.

On 15 June, a party of Crusaders entered the cave Church of St Peter's. A remarkable place of worship by any standards, the *Senpiyer Killisesi* – as it is known today – had been constructed in a huge grotto and was regarded as 'the world's first cathedral.' According to tradition, the place had belonged to St Luke the Evangelist and it was where St Peter had preached and used the term 'Christian' for the first time.

The party of diggers were understandably apprehensive – though they still hoped that if the spear were hidden there it would prove a good omen for the future. At the head of the group of twelve men – Peter had been instructed in his vision to take the same number as Jesus' apostles – were Count Raymond, a historian, Raymond of Aguilers who would record the event, and Peter himself.

The labourers worked hard for several hours, piling up sand and stones in ever increasing mounds, but without any success. Count Raymond finally grew tired of waiting for something to be unearthed and left the cave church, says Raymond of Aguilers. The historian continues in his journal:

Then Peter Bartholomew jumped into the hole to take a hand. He very soon cried out that he had found the lance. I touched the weapon while it still lay embedded in the ground. The spear was taken to Count Raymond, but Bishop Adhemar still refused to accept it as the real spear that had pierced the side of Christ. But so great was the rejoicing among the Crusaders when the news of this miracle was learned that he kept quiet.

To the desperate and hungry Crusaders, the discovery seemed like the sign they had been awaiting. A number of these men had heard the legend of the spear's power to influence destiny and of the remarkable victories its possessors had achieved during the past thousand years. Now, surely, was the time to ride out of Antioch and attack the infidel hordes?

There were still sceptics among the Crusaders, nonetheless, but their position was growing more hopeless by the day as famine ravaged their ranks. Outside the walls of Antioch, the men in the armies led by Sultan Kerbogha were also growing restless as they waited to attack. Some were even talking of leaving. When news of this dissension reached Count Raymond, he decided the moment had indeed come to go on the offensive.

Peter Bartholomew, who had never let the spear out of his sight since its discovery in the cave church, insisted that the Crusader army should take it with them when they advanced into the open. The date of the attack was set for 28 June and the outcome of this momentous day has been described by the anonymous author of a volume entitled *Documents des Croisades* (1780):

The Crusaders carried the holy lance on a standard at the head of the army. When Kerbogha saw the Crusaders in full array, he tried to send out for a truce, but the Crusaders still advanced. The Turks tried with their superior numbers to divide the Crusaders, but they kept in good formation. When Kerbogha saw this resolution on the faces of his enemy he feared that some of his emirs would desert the field of battle and so it happened. The first to retreat was Dukak of Damascus and soon Kerbogha's entire army collapsed. The Crusaders pressed hard and killed many of the fleeing Turks.

The victory spelt the end for Kerbogha and a triumph for the First Crusade. In renewed heart, Count Raymond and his men set off on the long and gruelling march south that involved them in several more battles and sieges before the army finally reached Jerusalem. There, in 1099, the Crusaders took the holy city and established the Latin Kingdom of Jerusalem as well as the orders of Knights Hospitallers and Knights Templars.

One man, however, did not live to see the culmination of the Crusade – the monk who had inspired the victory through his discovery of the spear. Accounts of Peter Bartholomew's death are, though, confused. One version claims that on the march from Antioch to Jerusalem he had repeated visions about the military tactics that should be employed against the enemy. These tested the patience of the more sceptical among Count Raymond's noblemen to the point that they finally demanded that the monk prove he was receiving divine inspiration. At this, he offered to undergo the biblical test of passing through a 'fiery furnace' to demonstrate his faith.

It is reported that Bartholomew did indeed walk between two walls of flame especially constructed by the Crusaders. Although the monk emerged still upright, he was seriously burned and died in agony some days later. A simpler version of his end says he died of sunstroke while crossing the fiery desert wastes of Syria.

The arguments as to whether the spear was genuine or not continued to rage long after Peter Bartholomew's death. The account of the man and his visions had as many supporters as detractors, as Richard Rainey has noted:

> Sceptics claimed that Count Raymond had conjured up the lance himself, even delivering the appropriate visions to the mystic Peter. But a lance was found – and whether it was a hoax or the real item, planted or discovered, the lance changed the course of history.

The fate of this particular spear is also a puzzle. Excavations in the 'world's first cathedral' beneath the remaining mosaic tiles on the floor and a painstaking study of a number of faded frescoes on the walls have yielded no clues. It has, though, been claimed that the lance was taken to Jerusalem by Count Raymond's Crusaders and there 'put in a place of honour'. If this was Mount Sion, then the Antioch story could be just another episode in the history of the spear that is now in St Peter's Church in Rome.

It has also been suggested that it might subsequently have found its way to Armenia – but this is certainly confusing the facts with the story to be related next. The truth is actually much simpler – and much more prosaic. M.F. De Mely in his classic work on the history of the spear has the answer: 'Scholars believe that it was not actually a Roman lance at all, but the head of a standard. Although it may have an interesting story of its own, this is quite separate from the Legend of the Lance.'

The story of the apostle St Paul' s travels through Asia Minor in AD36, sowing the seeds of Christianity and establishing the seven churches of Revelation is familiar enough to require only the briefest mention here. Journeying from Antioch through Cappadocia, he converted people all along his way, while at the same time angering the existing religions, especially the Jews. It would be 200 years, in fact, before the persecution of Christians began to wane with the conversion of the first king, Abgar VIII of Edessa, and the proselytising of Gregory 'The Illuminator' in Armenia. The history of the last and most important Spear of Longinus rests with this extraordinary man and the ancient land where he was born.

Armenia, land-locked in the Lesser Caucasus Mountains, has been described as one of the 'Cradles of Civilisation'. According to the *Book of Genesis*, Noah's Ark landed on the summit of Mount Ararat, the highest and most hallowed mountain, in the heart of the country (which is now part of Turkey). From the Ark, of course, Noah's descendants and all the species of animals and birds departed in pairs to populate the world.

Regardless of whether this story is true or not, there is no denying the long, tumultuous and often fantastic history of Armenia. Once upon a time its territory stretched from the Black Sea to the Caspian Sea and included much of what is now eastern Turkey and Iran – as the deserted Christian city of Ani in Turkey and the various Christian churches in Iran bear silent witness. Armenia was, in fact, the first extensive kingdom to adopt Christianity as a state religion and also to pioneer a type of architecture that anticipated the Gothic style of the West.

There are many legends about the coming of Christianity to Armenia, a land with a long tradition of being continually invaded by hostile neighbours of other faiths. Indeed, almost every spring in any narrow valley, and every battered wall surrounding an ancient church or monastery has a tale of faith, tragedy and often bloodshed to tell.

The oldest traditions in Armenia claim that Christianity was first taught in the country by the apostles – or at least their immediate disciples, especially St Bartholomew and St Thaddeus – but there is no contemporary evidence to support these reports. However, by the second century after the death of Christ, the religion bearing his name was certainly gathering followers in the regions bordering Armenia – in particular the apostolic churches in Antioch and Kayseri, which played important roles in the diffusion of the faith. The influence of these communities and the constant traffic of people between them were to pave the way for the arrival of Christianity.

Closest of all to Armenia was the ancient Christian centre of Edessa whose king, Abgar VIII, was to have a profound effect on the man who would become known as St Gregory the Illuminator, and who was responsible for the official conversion of the country in 1301 The story of this major figure in Armenia's history is told in a number of very old documents, frescoes and paintings – although there is still much that is not certain about the saint. The account by the historian, Faustus of Buzanda, is perhaps one of the most reliable sources of information.

Gregory, born Grigor Lusavorish, is described as a member of the Pathian noble house of Suren-Pahlev – a branch of the Arsacid royal family – and thus a kinsman of the Armenian monarchs. According to Faustus, Gregory's father assassinated the Armenian king, Khosrow, in 238, and as a consequence almost all his family were wiped out in retaliation. The child Gregory was the only one to escape the slaughter and was taken to neighbouring Cappadocia where he grew up as a Christian in Caesarea.

In 286 – says the historian – the Roman emperor Diocletian restored the son of the murdered King Khosrow to his ancestral kingdom, as King Tiridates III. Twelve years later, thanks to the Treaty of Nisibis, Armenia was recognised as an independent nation, albeit under Roman protection. On hearing this news, the exiled Gregory decided to return to his native land, bringing with him the message of Christianity – and a precious relic symbolic of the faith, the Spear of Longinus. Faustus continues his *Chronicle*:

> Gregory returned to the country of his fathers and began to preach the Christian faith. Tiridates discovered and identified him as the son of his own father's murderer. The King ordered him to suffer gruesome tortures after which Gregory was cast into a dungeon in the royal castle of Vagharashat, where he languished for fifteen years. A charitable widow saved his life and provided him with food.

According to the thirteenth-century Armenian historian, Vartan, in his *Historie des Croisades*, Gregory had in his possession a 'holy lance' that he had been given while he was in Caesarea. This was the spear that the Centurion Longinus had used to pierce the side of Christ and it remained in his possession throughout all the time he conducted his ministry in Kayseri.

Vartan believed that Longinus had lived for a time in the Goreme Valley, a spot where Christian monks would later settle in some numbers. It was here, too, that St Basil founded one of the earliest Christian monasteries and the church bearing his name. Inside this can still be seen the graves of the early monks and the eerie fingerprints of an unknown artist who painted the building's frescoes in the tenth century.

Longinus passed the weapon to one of his converts to use as 'a symbol of the blood of the Saviour spilt to save mankind'. From this man's hands, the Armenian historian says, it had passed to Gregory 'who revered it above all other relics of the Lord'.

Vartan also mentions a rumour that credited two other early Christians as possible carriers of the spear to Armenia – the apostle Matthew and Joseph of Arimathaea – but believes that there is no substantial evidence to dispute St Gregory's ownership.

Before his imprisonment by Tiridates, Gregory apparently hid the lance in a cave in the mountainous region of Kotayk, just to the east of the ancient town of Yerevan. It was here that for centuries before the arrival of Christianity, hermits had retreated from the world to take refuge in the region's many natural caves. These men had been among Gregory's first converts to

Christianity. Here, too, he would later found the country's first monastery.

The Christian preacher's imprisonment in the underground virap was brought to a dramatic end when the unruly and lecherous Tiridates ordered the brutal killing of a group of pious Christian women, including a particularly beautiful virgin, Hripsime, who had all refused to join the king's harem of wives and concubines. Armenian legend says the king was struck down by divine intervention and it was only when his sister, Khosrovidukht, told him of a vision she had had of a man 'with a radiant face' who was the only person who could save him, that the monarch agreed to release Gregory. Tiridates was immediately cured and was so grateful that he decided along with all his family to accept Christianity.

Gregory himself also had a vision not long after his release from the dungeon He saw the figure of Christ 'carrying a golden lance', according to the chronicler, Faustus of Buzanda, 'with which he struck the earth in the midst of the royal town of Vagharshapat'. A great column of fire arose from the spot, surmounted by a shining cross. This was followed by the appearance of four arches, a huge cupola and a golden throne all in the likeness of an enormous cathedral.

As a result of this vision that earned Gregory the title of 'The Illuminator', he built a reproduction of the 'mystical church' on the exact spot where he had seen the fiery column touch the ground He renamed the town as Echmiadzin, meaning 'The Only Begotten Descended'. The site itself was significant as it had for centuries been the location of a Zoroastrian fire temple – and indeed evidence of this pagan worship would later be discovered in a crypt. From 180 to 340, Etchmiadzin was the capital of Armenia.

This great church was not, though, Gregory's only creation in the country where he served as primate until his death in 325. In the canyon above the Azat River forty kilometres southeast of Yerevan, where he had made his first converts and left the spear of Longinus for safekeeping, he founded a cave church and monastery. Known originally as Ayrivank, 'the monastery of the caves', it was carved out of the soft stone of the valley and soon became the centre of a large monastic community.

The complex consisted of the *Ekklesia Katholike* for theological study; a *gavit* or holy retreat hollowed out of the steep cliffs on the north side of the monastery; and the *zhamatun*, or Hall of the Synod. Inside the enclosure, numerous other chapels and cells were also cut out of the rock, all of them on different levels of the mountain slope. Outside the walls to the west another chapel was hewn from the rock and consecrated as St Stvadzadzin, 'Mother of God'. Inside this striking place of worship a number of ancient inscriptions have recently been discovered, one of the oldest dating from 1164.

Known as St Basil's, this unique religious community soon began to attract Christians from far and wide. A tradition also developed amongst these pilgrims for tying strips of cloth to the trees that grew between the monastery and the river in order to bring them good luck. It was said that anyone who offered a prayer while fixing one of these pieces of linen to a branch would have their wish come true.

Tragically, however, disaster struck the community in 923 when Arabs invaded the country and destroyed much of the monastery. Luckily the spear hidden in its cave escaped destruction. In 1215, a new church, the *Astvatsatin* 'Virgin Mary' was constructed, complete with an adjoining vestibule that is larger than the church itself and contains nine arches and a magnificent carved ceiling. Several smaller chapels were also built into the rock side, one of which contains a holy spring whose waters are said to keep skin youthful.

The refurbished monastery was renamed after its most famous relic, Gheghardavank, meaning 'Monastery of the Holy Lance'. Here the spear would remain for several centuries after the Romans had left the country to its fate and its people had repeatedly suffered from Saracen raids and Byzantine interference. The lance was, in fact, soon being as jealously guarded by the Armenians as their Christian religion and their national heritage.

The great twelfth-century Armenian scholar and theologian, Archbishop Nerses of Lampron, mentions the holy lance and the veneration in which it is held on several occasions in the course of his voluminous writings. He refers to it being on display at a Synod at Ashtishat in 365 and makes an intriguing reference to the emperor Frederick Barbarossa who recruited a number of Armenian knights for the Third Crusade in 1189. Unfortunately, Nerses does not mention whether the German monarch was aware of this rival claimant to the holy spear he himself possessed – or make any speculation as to which might be the genuine one.

At some point during the seventh century, the cathedral at Etchmiadzin was rebuilt, including the construction of a beautiful treasury on the right hand side of the altar. (Later additions would also be made in 1654 and 1868.) Into this went the collection of illuminated manuscripts, richly embroidered vestments, golden chalices and jewelled crosses that had been gathered over the years – as well as the holy spear which had been brought from Gheghardavank.

It is here that the fragile and delicate treasures have been kept ever since, and special permission is required from the Armenian Church authorities to examine them. Notable among the items is the right hand of a saint enclosed in a silver case and a piece of wood said to have come from Noah's Ark. It was supposedly given to a thirteenth-century Armenian monk by an angel after the holy man had tried unsuccessfully three times to climb Mount Ararat. This sliver of wood was carbon dated some years ago and has been shown to be at least 6,000 years old.

No tests of any kind have, however, been permitted

c & d The spear of Etchmiadzin – and a cutaway key

by the church authorities on the lance and the photograph in this book is one of the most recent to have been taken. However, the diagram above of the relic and the explanation of its various component parts attests to its great age.

The symbol 'A' indicates the spearhead and 'B' a moulded cross added at a later date. 'C' marks a cross constructed of two pieces of metal that have been riveted to the back of the lance 'according to the tradition of the Apostle Saint Thomas'. It is stated in the notes that the spearhead is cracked diagonally – though this is not shown on the diagram – and held together by the crossed strips of metal. The attachments 'D' and 'E' are the red seal of a patriarch, Daniel, and the yellow seal of another patriarch, David, who both disputed for the supreme patriarchy of Armenia in 1805 and claimed the spear for their own. Even though the argument was settled in favour of Daniel, this date marks one of the last appearances of the holy relic in public.

Those scholars and experts on holy relics who have made the long trek to Etchmiadzin – now the headquarters of the Armenian Orthodox Church – are satisfied as to the great antiquity of the metal of the spearhead. Precisely whether or not it is the original Spear of Longinus is something, as M. de Mely has put it in his book, 'We shall probably never be certain.'

For myself, I believe that if any part of the Lance of Longinus has survived its long and tortuous journey through time, then this relic in Armenia is most probably the real one. However, the spear's final destiny after passing through the hands of so many people – good as well as evil – not forgetting its undoubted symbolic power and it true place in history, is still very far from being resolved.

Bibliography

Ananikian, M.H., *Armenian Mythology*, Boston Books, 1925

Angeburt, Jean-Michel, *The Occult and the Third Reich*, McGraw Hill, 1983

Baring-Gould, Sabine, *The Lives of the Saints*, John Grant, 1914

Bible – the Gospels of St Matthew, St Luke, St Mark and St John, CUP

Brennan, J.H., *Occult Reich*, Futura Publications Ltd, 1974

Brewer, E.Cobham, *Dictionary of Phrase and Fable*, London, 1894

Buechner, Howard A. & Bernhart, Wilhelm, *Adolf Hitler and the Secrets of the Holy Lance*, Thunderbird Press Inc., 1989

Bullock, Alan, *Hitler, A Study in Tyranny*, Harper & Row, 1964

Conybeare, F.C., *The Key of Truth*, Oxford University Press, 1898

De Mely, F., *Exuviae Sacre Constantopolilonae*, Leroux, 1804

Fishman, Jack, *The Seven Men of Spandau*, W.H.Allen, 1954

Freely, John B., *The Companion Guide to Turkey*, Collins, 1979

Gurney, O.R. *The Hittites*, Penguin Books, 1968

Howe, Ellic, *Urania's Children*, William Kimber, 1970

Inglisian, Vahan, *Armenia and the Bible*, Vienna, 1935

Khanzadian, Emma, *The Culture of the Armenian Highlands*, Erevan, 1967

King, Francis, *Satan and Swastika*, Granada Publishing, 1976

Kolosimo, Peter, *Not Of This World*, Sphere, 1970

Kyle, Duncan, *Black Camelot*, St Martin's Press Inc., 1978

Lloyd, Seton, *Early Anatolia*, Penguin Books, 1956

Macler, F., *Légendes Populaires d'Arménie*, Paris, 1933

Mango, Cyril, *Byzantine Architecture*, Harry N. Abrams., 1976

Mathews, John, *The Grail and the Quest for Eternal Light*, Thames & Hudson, 1981

Mellaart, James, *Earliest Civilisations for the Near East*, Thames & Hudson, 1965

Muller-Weiner, W., *Castle of the Crusaders*, Collins, 1966

Paulin, P., *La Chanson d'Antioche*, Techner, 1848

Pauwels, Louis & Bergier, Jacques, *The Dawn of Magic*, Gibbs & Phillips, 1963; reprinted as *The Morning of Magicians*, Souvenir Press, 2000

Pennick, Nigel, *Hitler's Secret Sciences*, Neville Spearman, 1981

Peters, F.E., *The Harvest of Hellenism*, Simon & Schuster, 1970

Rainey, Richard, *Phantom Forces*, Berkely Books, 1990

Ravenscroft, Trevor, *The Spear of Destiny*, Neville Spearman, 1973

— & Wallace-Murphy, Tim, *The Mark of The Beast*, Sphere, 1990

Rice, Tamara, *The Seljuks in Asia Minor*, Thames & Hudson, 1961

Rodley, Lyn, *Cave Monasteries of Byzantine Cappadocia*, Cambridge University Press, 1986

Runciman, Steven, *The Fall of Constantinople*, Cambridge University Press, 1965

Shirer, William L., *The Rise and Fall of the Third Reich*, Simon & Schuster, 1960

Sprater, Friedrich, *Die Reichskleinodien in der Pfalz*, Ludwigshafen, 1942

Stein, Walter Johannes, *The Ninth Century and the Holy Grail*, Temple Lodge Press, 1988

Steiner, Rudolf, *The Mysteries of the East and Christianity*, Steiner Press, 1972

Toland, John, *Hitler*, Ballantine Books, 1970

Trevor-Roper, Hugh, *The Last Days of Adolf Hitler*, Macmillan, 1945

Walker, Warren S., *Tales Alive in Turkey*, Harvard University Press, 1966